FRIENDSHIP
SIGNS

Your Perfect Match(es) Are in the Stars

Brianne Hogan

ADAMS MEDIA

NEW YORK LONDON TORONTO SYDNEY NEW DELHI

To my friends: Andrea (Virgo), Brandon (Virgo), Colin
(Gemini), Davina (Sagittarius), Elena (Scorpio), Katie
(Leo), Lauren (Scorpio), Linda (Aries), Mariko (Virgo),
Monica (Aries), Rob (Capricorn), and Stu (Taurus).
And to best friends: Mom (Aries) and Dad (Pisces).

Aadamsmedia

Adams Media
An Imprint of Simon & Schuster, Inc.
57 Littlefield Street
Avon, Massachusetts 02322

First Adams Media hardcover edition May 2019

ADAMS MEDIA and colophon are trademarks of Simon & Schuster.

For information about special discounts for bulk purchases,
please contact Simon & Schuster Special Sales at 1-866-506-1949
or business@simonandschuster.com.

The Simon & Schuster Speakers Bureau can bring authors to your live event.
For more information or to book an event contact the Simon & Schuster
Speakers Bureau at 1-866-248-3049 or visit our website at
www.simonspeakers.com.

Interior images by Claudia Wolf; © Getty Images/MicrovOne

Manufactured in the United States of America

10 9 8 7 6 5 4 3 2 1 .

Library of Congress Cataloging-in-Publication Data has been applied for.

ISBN 978-1-5072-1022-2
ISBN 978-1-5072-1023-9 (ebook)

Contents

Introduction

It is said that friends are the family you choose. And where would you be without your friends? They help celebrate your victories, support you in your traumas and dramas, and always make you laugh. They lend their shoulders for you to cry on, their ears for when you need to vent, and their beautiful hearts to shower you with love. Your friendships help give meaning to your life, allowing you to feel connected to the world around you in deep, intimate ways. So how do you know when you've met the peanut butter to your jelly? Better still, how can you further understand the friendships you have now? You could say that it's written in the stars.

Astrology helps you gain a better understanding of who you are and how you relate to the world around you—specifically within your relationships with others. Every zodiac sign carries a unique energy, which can either connect to or repel your own astrological energy. Understanding someone's Sun sign will give you a personal guide to cultivating a happy, lasting friendship. In *Friendship Signs*, you'll discover things that you may not have known about a friend, such as how they handle conflict, what their friendship values are, and whether or not their idea of a fun Saturday night aligns with yours. As you read the "Friendship Compatibility" sections, keep in mind that many different combinations of Sun signs have experienced lifelong friendships. Sun signs tell only a portion of the story. Likewise, if you find a friend who isn't listed as a potential friendship match on your compatibility chart, trust your instincts.

You will also notice in this book that each sign has several recurring aspects. A sign has a gender (male or female) and an element (water, fire, air, or earth). Water and earth signs are considered female, and air and fire signs are considered male. In addition to its element, each sign is categorized as one of three qualities: cardinal, fixed, or mutable. The cardinal signs begin each season; the fixed signs occur at the height of the season; and the mutable signs signal the change of one season to the next. Finally, each sign has a ruling planet that exemplifies the characteristics of the sign.

The two planets linked to friendship are Venus and Jupiter. Venus, or Aphrodite in ancient Greek mythology, is the goddess of love and inspires how you feel toward others. Jupiter, or Zeus, is the chief god of Roman and Greek mythology, and inspires how you show your emotions. Everyone has Venus and Jupiter located in a sign in their birth chart, and the placement of each planet will describe the yin and yang, or receptive and assertive, dynamic in your life.

Maybe you'll use this book to befriend that interesting person in your yoga class, or to gain a deeper awareness of a connection you already share with a close friend. Or maybe you just want to figure out what to buy your picky Virgo friend for her birthday. No matter your reason, you'll appreciate the unique friendship styles and qualities each sign has to offer.

Friendship
Compatibility Quiz

The following friendship compatibility quiz will help shine a light on your current friendships, and open the door to potential new friendships as well. Your answers will reveal insights about your personality and which sign may be the perfect friendship match for you. It's the moment of truth: are they friend or foe? Keep in mind that this quiz isn't the end-all, be-all of your friendship potential. If you share a close kinship with a sign that is not listed in your top three, it just means that there's a lot more to be explored within your charts. Remember this: there is no wrong answer!

1. **What qualities are most important to you in a friendship?**
   a Loyalty and trustworthiness
   b Adventurousness and spontaneity
   c Wit and intelligence
   d Empathy and supportiveness

2. **What is your favorite activity to do with a friend?**

   a Exploring the great outdoors
   b Going to a concert
   c Enjoying dinner at the latest hot spot
   d Watching favorite movies

3. **What is the one thing you could never forgive a friend for doing?**

   a Forgetting your birthday
   b Embarrassing you at a work function
   c Befriending your frenemy
   d Dating your ex

4. **When faced with a life-changing decision, how do you handle it?**

   a Create a pros and cons list
   b Do what feels right in the moment
   c Consider the interests of everyone involved
   d Meditate and use your intuition as your guide

5. **What is your favorite season?**

   a Autumn
   b Summer
   c Spring
   d Winter

6. If you could choose one face emoji to describe yourself, what would it be?

   a Cold sweat downcast face
   b Sunglasses smiley face
   c Smirking smiley face
   d Hugging smiley face

7. Which TV show genre would you most want to binge-watch?

   a Romantic drama
   b Action and adventure
   c Mystery
   d Sci-fi

8. Where would you most like to travel with your best friend?

   a Rome
   b New York City
   c London
   d Maui, Hawaii

9. What makes you LOL?

   a A heavy dose of sarcasm
   b Silly slapstick
   c Witty wordplay
   d Self-deprecating storytelling

10. How do you react when a friend cries in front of you?

   a Offer them advice
   b Try to make them laugh
   c Try to change the subject
   d Give them a hug

11. Which gift would be at the top of your birthday wish list?

   a A designer watch
   b A plush robe
   c A smartphone case
   d A diary

12. How do you typically handle a conflict?

   a Tackle it methodically, seeking advice from others
   b Confront it head-on
   c Ignore it until you have to deal with it
   d Shoulder the blame in order to resolve it as quickly as possible

13. Which is your favorite friendship keepsake from your childhood?

   a A friendship bracelet or cuff
   b A Little League trophy
   c A BFF necklace
   d A photo scrapbook

14. **What is your favorite snack for movie night?**

    a Cheese and crackers
    b Chips and guacamole
    c Popcorn
    d Ice cream

15. **You're working on a group project. Which role do you assume?**

    a The treasurer
    b The team captain
    c The publicist
    d The graphic designer

16. **What is your favorite genre of music?**

    a Jazz
    b Classic rock
    c Hip-hop
    d Pop

17. **Which literary genre do you prefer to read?**

    a Historical nonfiction
    b Adventure
    c Murder mystery
    d Romance

18. **What is your favorite act of self-care following an upsetting event?**

    a Attending a movie night with your nearest and dearest

    b Hitting up a yoga class with a friend to sweat out the feels

    c Checking out trivia night at the local dive bar with your best pal

    d Indulging in a day of pampering with your BFF

19. **What's your biggest pet peeve?**

    a When your plans are canceled at the last minute

    b When your text message is ignored

    c When you're put on hold for a long time

    d When you're told the word *no*

20. **If you won the lottery, what would be the first thing you do with the money?**

    a Spend a little, save a lot

    b Go on a globe-trotting adventure

    c Buy a new car

    d Splurge on new clothes

21. Group chat. You down?

    a If it serves a specific purpose, yes; otherwise, nope
    b I created the group chat
    c Only if I can use a ton of wildly inappropriate GIFs
    d Yes, and I speak only in emojis

22. What is your favorite holiday?

    a Christmas
    b New Year's Eve
    c Halloween
    d Easter

23. What form of exercise do you enjoy?

    a Hiking
    b Cycling
    c Yoga
    d Swimming

24. How would you describe your communication style?

    a I'm deliberate, thoughtful, and tend to think before I speak
    b I always speak my mind, and most times I have no filter
    c I can be a little scattered when I talk; I like to cover as much ground as possible
    d I always speak from my heart, and I can usually read between the lines

25. Which sitcom personality do you most relate to?

    a The mature, nurturing one

    b The sarcastic, rebellious one

    c The flirty, adventurous one

    d The sweet, lovable one

26. You're at a baseball game. What are you doing?

    a Nothing, because you don't go to baseball games

    b Playing ball

    c Eating

    d Cheering on the team, of course

27. What's your biggest fear?

    a Not living up to your own expectations

    b Your hard work going unnoticed

    c Having your independence taken away

    d Being alone

28. What is your stance on selfies?

    a Nah

    b I'm taking one right now

    c If I feel like it, sure

    d Only for special occasions

29. How would you direct a friend to comfort you when you're upset?

    a Help me talk it out when I'm ready
    b Bring me a punching bag
    c Validate my feelings
    d Let me cry it out

30. How do you prefer to keep in contact with your friends?

    a Texting mostly, sometimes a phone call
    b Video chat
    c A specific chat app
    d In person

31. You're on a road trip with your friends. What are you doing?

    a Navigating
    b Driving
    c Cracking jokes
    d Sleeping

32. How do you like to spend your spare time?

    a Volunteering
    b Working out
    c Exploring
    d Journaling

33. **It's your monthly dinner date with your friends. What would you prefer?**

    a An elaborate three-course dinner at a fancy restaurant

    b A slice of pizza at your place

    c The latest fusion food trend

    d A *Pinterest*-inspired home-cooked meal

34. **What's a simple way a friend can make you feel special?**

    a Sending you a "How's your day going?" text

    b Giving you their full attention

    c Telling you something they appreciate about you

    d Giving you a hug

35. **Which do you think is your most admirable quality?**

    a Dependability

    b Honesty

    c Humor

    d Sensitivity

Scoring

a = 4 points   b = 3 points   c = 2 points   d = 1 point

Add up your points for all thirty-five questions and check your results to find your most compatible friendship signs in the following chart.

Most Compatible Signs

Score	Your Best Friends	Other Potential Friends
101–140	Taurus, Virgo, or Capricorn	Cancer, Scorpio, or Pisces
71–100	Aries, Leo, or Sagittarius	Gemini, Libra, or Aquarius
51–70	Gemini, Libra, or Aquarius	Aries, Leo, or Sagittarius
35–50	Cancer, Scorpio, or Pisces	Taurus, Virgo, or Capricorn

Now that you know which signs are your friendship matches, flip to the relevant chapters to discover more about each sign match, from how they like to spend their time to how their friendship can enrich your life. You may even want to think back to what went wrong in past friendships and, with a little help from astrology, learn how you might prevent friendship conflicts in the future. More than anything, have fun exploring the unique friendships offered in each zodiac sign.

Chapter 1

Aries

(March 21–April 19)

Have a friend who owns the room the second they enter it? Chances are your friend is an Aries. Ruled by Mars, the planet of action and desire, Aries is a natural-born leader. However, Mars also represents aggression, which explains why Aries is quick to anger, but also why he is fiercely protective of his loved ones. Once you are a part of his trusted cavalry, Aries will gladly go to war for you.

The Leader

The first sign of the zodiac, Aries likes to rule the roost. Adventurous, open to change, and keen to initiate new ventures to ensure he is constantly moving and evolving, it comes as no surprise that Aries is happiest when he is running the show. Whether it's initiating a fantastic vacation, a college reunion, or a lovely hangout at home, your Aries friend will think up new and exciting things for you to try together.

Aries is also a cardinal sign, which means he was born at the start of a new season (spring). As a cardinal sign, he endows a strong will for setting things in motion, which along with his position as the first zodiac sign creates a double whammy of leadership qualities for your Aries buddy. You can always rely on Aries to come up with a plan of action, so if life becomes too overwhelming for you, your Aries friend will step up to make it easier on you. For example, if you're stressed out from moving apartments, Aries will figure out how to make it happen—and then delegate his plan out to others, like the true boss he is.

However forceful his personality is, your Aries friend will inspire you to uncover your ultimate potential. He will support any endeavor you embark upon for your personal growth, and you can count on him to be the first to arrive at the launch party of your side hustle (Aries always has to be first for everything, after all).

The Firecracker

Aries is fiery all right, and you can thank his natural element of fire for that. Like fire itself, fire signs are passionate, vital, and larger than life. This no doubt describes your Aries friend. However, while his strong personality can come off as, well, strong, Aries's infectious optimism helps to balance out his type A tendencies. No matter what life throws at him, it's natural for Aries to see the glass as half full. When the going gets tough, your Aries friend will help you see the bright side of your situation, not because he has his head in the sand—he is far too instinctive—but because he realizes there is always a lesson to be learned, especially from life's disappointments.

Aries is the friend who will send you inspiring texts to lift your spirits following a breakup, while also making sure you treat yourself to a night of fun. His vivacious energy not only makes him a joy to be around, but also lights the fire under you so you can do whatever it takes to boost your mood and improve your life. He'll motivate you to kick-start that new fitness routine (probably because he is leading the class) and push you to finally take that trip to Tokyo you've been talking about forever.

Aries Quirks: The Keeping-It-Real Ram

Symbolized by the ram, Aries not only is made to climb great heights, but also charges headfirst into everything in life, and most times he does so without thinking. His impulsiveness predisposes him with a prescription for tough love for whatever is happening in your life. Nope, the ram has no problem with telling you like it is. If Aries doesn't like your outfit, he will tell you. If Aries doesn't like the person you're dating, he'll tell you that too. He shoots from the hip in the name of honesty.

Unfortunately, Aries's sharpshooting ways often lack tact and diplomacy. There's no malice intended, but it's easy for feelings to be hurt. If you need some TLC, you might want to text your Pisces pal instead. However, if you need to hear the hard truth about a situation, Aries is the friend for the job. He prides himself on his ability to cut through the crap to get to the other side. If you're wavering on whether or not you should quit your boring job or break up with your equally boring partner, Aries has no problem telling you what to do (which will probably involve ditching either the job, partner, or both). After all, he knows that getting to the truth of the matter leads to a new level of success, and he's all about succeeding.

When you do message your ram friend about your issues, keep in mind that he can also have a "me first" attitude. Aries is naturally self-oriented and it's easy for him to get so wrapped up in what's going on in his own life that he forgets about everything else. So try not to take it personally if your Aries friend brings a conversation back to himself and his problems, or skips out on a Friday-night dinner to finish up a work project. Aries's striving and competitive nature means he has an endless energy to complete what needs to get done in order to move ahead to help ensure his success.

Bravado, Boredom, and a Big Heart

Aries's intense energy also means he has trouble sitting still. He craves adventure and challenges that will keep him stimulated and busy. If you would prefer a quiet night in or a vacation that includes lots of lounging, don't be surprised if Aries chooses a different option. He wants to be where the people are, and where there are new mountains (figurative or literal) to climb. The upside is that he will entice you to try these new things with him, which means he will be able to convince you to get off your couch and go to a concert on a Saturday night. The downside? If you balk, he'll probably leave you at home.

Aries's allergic reaction to boredom often brings out his impulsive side, causing him to make decisions that he may regret (but won't admit to) later. It's common for Aries to act and speak before thinking things through. If something seems too extreme for your tastes, let the ram do his thing alone.

However, if you can keep up with the insatiable energy of Aries, then you better believe you will have a friend for life. Aries is passionate about everything, including his friendships. Your Aries friend is extremely generous with his time, energy, and money. This ram likes to share what he has learned in order to help his nearest and dearest succeed. He will sit with you for hours to talk out an issue—leading the conversation and dispensing advice, of course—and will even help you construct a game plan. He wants to be the friend who guides you to becoming your best self. Aries will go above and beyond for his tribe, often picking up the check at lunch or throwing you a giant birthday bash. Know that underneath his bravado lies a huge heart.

Leading the Pack: Where You'll Meet Aries

From improv class to skiing to mountain climbing, Aries craves adventure and being where he will get noticed. Thanks to his assertive vibe, there's little doubt that Aries will end up running the show soon after joining a new club or organization. Are you taking a fitness class? Aries is probably the cycling instructor (or will be soon). Attending an acting workshop? Aries easily slides into the role of the director. But his desire for the spotlight doesn't come from an egotistical place: Aries prefers to lead because he truly believes he can motivate those around him—also because he thinks he is the only one for the job.

As Aries values success, he will also spend his time volunteering, attending workshops, or at networking events—doing whatever he can to ensure he is getting a leg up on the competition.

You will definitely notice the Aries in the room, because he is energetically leading the charge, as well as delegating what needs to be done.

Letting Him Come to You: How to Become Friends with Aries

At heart, Aries is independent and likes to do his thing, especially if you meet him at work or at an activity he loves. Intruding on his space, like interrupting him while he's clearly leading the charge or being honored for his many achievements, will only turn him off. If Aries sees friend potential in you, allow him to initiate contact. Once he does, be ready for a flurry of questions as he sizes you up. "What do you do for a living?" and "How do you let off steam?" are common Aries questions. Aries wants to know whether you can keep up with him both physically and intellectually. Prove that you're up for an adventure—as well as able to hold your own in a conversation with him—and he will welcome you into his inner circle.

Because of his need to lead a given situation, being easygoing jibes best with his more assertive vibe. For example, when he starts directing your entire Friday night out, don't take offense; instead, try to see it as a compliment. Taking charge of a situation is part of Aries's nature, but it's also how he demonstrates his affection. When he takes the reins of your weekend vacation, it's important to know that his heart is in the right place. No wonder calling "shotgun" is music to his ears.

Untrustworthy and Clingy: Aries Friendship Dislikes

Aries doesn't do clingy. Anyone reeking of neediness will be shown the door—or will be just plain ignored. He needs his friends to respect his space, which means no incessant texting or calling, or repeatedly asking, "Where's the party at?" Don't worry; if Aries wants you to know where the next shindig is, he will tell you. Your Aries friend also doesn't like taking orders or being dictated to, which, yes, is a bit ironic considering that's exactly what Aries does. But that's just how he rolls. Aries also doesn't have time for anyone who breaks his code of trust. To the ferocious warrior Aries—ruled by Mars, also known in Roman mythology as the god of war—commitment means everything. He needs to trust you to have his back, especially when the going gets tough. Fool him once, and there won't be a second chance.

Fire and Fury: How Aries Handles Conflict

Aries's temper is fierce. Hotheaded doesn't even begin to describe him. He is intensely reactive and often suffers from blind rage. In an instant, he can cut you down to the quick with his searing words—that is, he's not above indulging in a childlike temper tantrum when things don't go his way. Aries hates to lose, especially in arguments, which is unfortunate, because his impulsive nature may cost him dear friendships. If you go to battle with your Aries friend, be prepared to lose the argument—and possibly the friendship—as Aries struggles to swallow his pride and take ownership for his part in an argument. It's best to refrain from a war of words and to stop engaging immediately during a conflict. Give Aries space to cool off and sort out his feelings. When he comes back to you, allow him to take his natural lead in the conversation. Accept his apology and move on quickly.

Motivation and Understanding: Maintaining Your Friendship with Aries

Underneath his confident outer armor lies a sign who at times can feel quite insecure. Aries works hard because, deep down, he may believe he's not worthy of the success he desires. Offering Aries words of encouragement and support from time to time will help him, especially when you sense he is struggling. Remind him of his past accomplishments and motivate him to keep climbing, just as he motivates you. Keep in mind that Aries will seldom admit to his troubles, so it's key to listen to your intuition and go with your gut when feeling out Aries's needs.

Another thing to consider is that Aries's worst fear is being forgotten, especially by those who matter most to him. One way to combat that fear is to bring your problems to your Aries friend. Seriously. There is nothing that makes the ram feel more wanted than a friend who seeks his counsel. He loves giving his time, advice, and sympathy—so vent away.

On the other hand, your Aries friend craves a lot of space. Sometimes this is difficult to accept, particularly if you're the type of person who gains energy from being around your friends. Understand that this is nothing personal—it's just part of the Aries's independent nature. Simply wait it out until your Aries friend calls you again with information on a new adventure he would love to embark upon with you. Accepting Aries's need for alone time is one of the best gifts you can give him.

Last but not least, try not to take Aries's fiery personality personally. He can be unintentionally forceful and combative, much like his animal symbol, which can make some people feel defensive or intimidated. Don't be afraid to speak your mind, but also know that Aries means no harm. If you can let Aries take the lead, understanding that is simply his role in your friendship dynamic, your friendship will flourish.

BFF Bonus Points

When it comes to gifts, Aries loves anything that looks and feels powerful. Consider a new tech gadget, like the latest video game or smartphone. You can also entertain his playful and active side by treating him to tickets to a baseball game, new workout clothing, or a piece of sports equipment.

Friendship Compatibility

So, will Aries and Taurus be friends forever? What can Aries expect from a friendship with Sagittarius? In the following section, you'll get the scoop on Aries's astrological compatibility with each Sun sign.

Aries and Aries

Double dare alert. When two Aries come together, it's bound to be a 24/7 adventure. Who else will go on an impromptu road trip with Aries or race him to the top of, well, anything? It's helpful if the two rams view each other as teammates, so they'll burn brightly with inspiration, rather than blazing with fiery competition. If they don't burn each other out, they're in for a thrilling ride. Just beware of arguments: since the ram is known for his volatile temper, two rams fighting will be downright explosive.

Aries and Taurus

While the laissez-faire vibe of peacekeeping Taurus can be a calming influence on Aries, Aries may feel annoyed at times with his sluggish bull friend. Aries likes to charge ahead, and Taurus prefers to take a nap, which can make things a bit frustrating, especially when it comes to Friday dinner plans. And speaking of dinner, Taurus likes to stick to her old haunts, while Aries is always ready to taste something new. Seeing the good in each other and being flexible will help this friendship last longer than a meal.

Aries and Gemini

Gemini has both the energy and the love of adventure to keep up with Aries. This twin will gladly hold the ram's hand as they jump out of a plane together. No plan of action is too daring for Gemini. However, Gemini's frenetic pace might become too scattered for laser-focused Aries, and Gemini might find Aries too bossy at times. Giving each other space sometimes will be a good idea. One thing's for sure: they'll never be bored with each other.

Aries and Cancer

As an emotional water sign protected by a hard outer shell, Cancer is difficult for Aries to read. Aries longs to get the crab out of her shell, but thanks to her homebody tendencies, she won't respond well to his requests—which no doubt ruffles Aries's feathers. Respecting each other's different energies and acknowledging the unique gifts each person brings to the relationship is key in keeping this friendship strong. If Aries can learn from Cancer's vulnerability and Cancer can take Aries's forcefulness with a grain of salt, their friendship will flourish.

Aries and Leo

BFF alert. These two fire signs are all about adventure, and they both have the high energy to explore each new experience that comes their way. Thanks to a healthy dose of competition, there will never be a dull moment between these friends. Leo engages the more playful side of Aries, helping him to lighten up and see that fun doesn't have to be so intense. At the same time, Aries helps turn the lavish dreams of the lion into reality. If Leo can overlook Aries's bossiness and Aries can see past Leo's vanity, this will be a powerful friendship for the ages.

Aries and Virgo

The intelligent and grounded Virgo doesn't play into fiery Aries's need to pull rank. Showmanship doesn't impress the practical virgin, which irritates Aries. Virgo's need to analyze and rationalize each commitment and activity can also annoy Aries, since he prefers to live in the moment. Virgo's slow and steady vibe can clash with Aries's impulsiveness, while Aries's trademark brashness can be off-putting to the always-modest Virgo. However, Aries needs a bit of stability, which Virgo can provide, and Virgo needs to let loose once in a while, and Aries is ready to help her do just that. This friendship will take a lot of patience.

Aries and Libra

While Libra is the astrological opposite to Aries, this is a friendship that has the potential to provide balance—which is especially great since Libra is all about balance. Aries and Libra are both social creatures, so they enjoy going out together, mingling, and painting the town red. Both talkative people, they easily get lost in conversation with each other. Libra's flakiness has the potential to offend Aries, however, while Aries's incessant pushiness can turn off Libra. But accepting each other's quirks will help this friendship blossom.

Aries and Scorpio

Scorpio's a natural daredevil like Aries, which makes choosing activities easy for this pair. However, as both of these signs are ruled by Mars, Aries and Scorpio are passionate people who are prone to temper tantrums and spurts of selfishness. These two will either be allies or mortal enemies. Fortunately, both Aries and Scorpio also like to encourage each other to live their best lives, so if they can share rank and look past their blowouts, they will have a blast (of fun) together.

Aries and Sagittarius

This duo is full of fun: they both share a high energy and craving for adventure. From hitting the gym together to planning the next vacation, they're always up for a good time and like to keep busy. Basically, they're best buddies. That is, as long as Aries can appreciate Sagittarius's need to travel alone sometimes, and Sagittarius can tolerate Aries's need to take charge of the trip.

Aries and Capricorn

Competitive and ambitious, this pair may face a number of obstacles in their friendship. However, Capricorn is supportive of Aries's talents and Aries trusts Capricorn's instincts, which gives this duo killer potential. With the sea goat's undying loyalty and the ram's inspiring energy, these two have the power to take over the world. If they can continue to encourage and trust each other, rather than see each other as the competition, their friendship will be for life.

Aries and Aquarius

Aries and Aquarius can challenge each other in spectacular ways. Benevolent Aquarius can help Aries put the world's problems before his own, while Aries can help put the wildest ideas of Aquarius into action. They both care deeply about humanity, so they can spend time volunteering together for a charity that's dear to them, or work on a project that they believe can help change the world. One glitch? Aries won't like Aquarius's indecisiveness, while Aquarius will have a hard time with Aries's temper. However, if these two are able to accept each other's differences, they can end up doing a lot of good for humanity.

Aries and Pisces

Aries's boldness is almost too much for sensitive Pisces to bear, while Aries has a hard time accepting the thoughtful and intuitive rhythm of Pisces. The homebody nature of Pisces will annoy Aries, and the bravado of Aries is a turnoff for the fish. If these two can learn to appreciate each other's strengths, they can learn a lot from each other. Aries could learn to tap into his sensitivity from Pisces, and Pisces can learn to stand up for herself from the ram. However, this friendship could very well be dead in the water if they don't make an effort.

Friendship Planets: Venus and Jupiter

Looking at where Venus and Jupiter are in your friend's and your charts, in addition to your Sun signs, can further help you understand that friend and your relationship with them. Venus rules love and unions of all kinds, including friendships. Its location in your birth chart reflects *how* you love. Jupiter, meanwhile, is the planet of optimism, success, and generosity, and indicates how you *show* your love to those close to you.

Venus in Aries

When Venus is in Aries, he abides by the principle of tough love—it's basically his bumper sticker of life. Friends know they can count on him to deliver the hard truth of any situation because he cares so much.

Venus in Aries is notoriously impulsive and always up for a challenge, which means he likes to keep busy and usually has a knack for making fast friends who are as assertive and independent as he is. He thrives on activity and hopes that by continuously challenging himself, he can inspire his friends to reach new heights of their own.

A generous person, Venus in Aries loves to surprise his friends with gifts and thoughtful text messages. However, he also demands a lot of time and attention from his friends, which can be daunting for some. Of course, he doesn't consider himself challenging—it's just that he doesn't have time for fake friends.

Jupiter in Aries

Jupiter in Aries is confident and not afraid to lead a crowd. Thanks to his larger-than-life personality, he has the ability to win over a number of different people, but he also has a tendency to be a bit of a bully and a know-it-all. The independent nature of Jupiter in Aries can make it hard for others to warm up to him, and his brashness can intimidate some friends. It's important for Jupiter in Aries to welcome his friends' ideas with an open mind. He is his best self when he is able to inspire friends by modeling courage, rather than by bossing them around. His innate enthusiasm, not his need for control, is what draws friends to him like moths to a flame.

Chapter 2

Taurus

(April 20–May 20)

Once you're a friend of Taurus, you're a friend for life. Like her symbol, the bull, Taurus is strong, determined, and, yes, a little stubborn—meaning once she has let you into her inner circle, there is no turning back.

The Voice of Reason

Taurus is an earth sign, and while your bull friend undoubtedly likes nice things and has penchant for being materialistic, her natural element also represents emotions and the value you place on the people closest to you. Earthy Taurus reminds the rest of the world that everything in life starts with a solid foundation—a foundation partly comprised of the relationships you have with others, including friendships. As faithful and stable as her element suggests, Taurus is committed to sticking by the people closest to her through good times *and* bad times. This is why Taurus is so picky when selecting her squad: she only wants to surround herself with the best quality of friends. In fact, quality over quantity wins out every time for Taurus. From friendships to fashion, she knows the difference between a flash in the pan and the real deal. She only craves what will go the distance.

The inherent practicality of Taurus is also due in part to her being a fixed sign. This means she was born at the height of a season (spring), and is influenced by stability, focus, and perseverance. As a fixed sign, Taurus is the perfect person to turn to when any kind of calamity occurs. Even if you've messed up big-time, whether it's a fight with your family or burning the holiday dinner, Taurus will not leave your side. She will always give you the soundest advice, covering every logistic possible. As a fixed sign, her persistent, slow-and-steady vibe will help you see the bigger picture and ensure you concentrate on taking things one step at a time.

The Nurturer

Taurus's ruling planet Venus instills an innate need for growth and development among her connections with loved ones, which also explains why she is all about creating a solid foundation for her friendships. Since Venus is the planet of love, Taurus longs for peace and harmony within her tribe. She is interested in seeking out happy friendships that make use of the simple pleasures in life, like going out for a hike or spending time indoors cooking a fantastic meal—anything that enhances an easy connection. She is also only interested in friendships that go the distance and thus works hard to establish trust and loyalty with her friends.

Sweet-natured and compassionate (a hallmark of her planetary ruler), she loves tending to the little details when it comes to celebrating and being there for you. It's safe to say your Taurus pal never forgets your birthday or "friendiversary." Chances are the gifts she surprises you with are also immensely personal and probably DIY, like a scrapbook of your most treasured memories together. When it comes to getting together, Taurus doesn't mind if Taco Tuesday happens at her favorite restaurant or *chez toi*. All that matters is that you are spending time together—and that there's food (this epicurean bull does love to eat). And while Taurus is inherently clever and has a great sense of humor, she insists upon her friends taking the spotlight, and will gladly sit back to watch you shine. Your Taurus friend will never judge you; she accepts and loves you for you.

Taurus Quirks: The Bullheaded Bull

It should come as no surprise that your Taurus friend can be as stubborn as, well, a bull. She is very fixed in her ways (which, as a fixed sign, isn't a shocker either), and trying to change her mind is nearly impossible. Being so headstrong, it takes her a long time to make any decision, so if she's already decided on what you're eating and doing on this Saturday night get-together, good luck convincing her otherwise.

And speaking of change, Taurus hates it. This bull is a natural-born creature of habit, needing a lot of stability in every aspect of her life. She will dig in her heels as much, and for as long, as possible until things go her way. It's easy, then, to see why Taurus can come across as selfish at times, as her stubbornness means she will protect her own interests at all costs.

When working on a group project, Taurus (as the raring bull that she is) doesn't mind taking charge. She'll eagerly take up a task and won't rest until it's completed. However, she may struggle to multitask, as she likes what she likes and doesn't want to be bothered by details outside of that specific task. This can lead to a habit of procrastinating, and may also prompt her to defer to you (or whoever else is involved) as the "boss," because she doesn't wish to take on any more responsibility. While some might call her sluggish at times, she just doesn't see the utility in going beyond her call of duty if it isn't necessary. In order to help motivate your Taurus friend, you might remind her of the potential financial gains of a project (she does love having money in the bank). Since Taurus is also a pleasure-seeker, suggesting that she reward herself for a job well done with a deep massage or box of chocolates could also be the ticket to her success.

Control Freak and Creature of Comfort

Your Taurus friend's down-to-earth personality means she loves comfort more than anything, especially when it comes to her surroundings. She is famous for her "vegging out" skills, routinely raiding your fridge for snacks and opting for a movie night on the couch over a night out. Persuading her with dinner at her favorite go-to restaurant can help you get her off the couch, because if she can't *be* at home, she will definitely want to *feel* at home. However, when Taurus is in the mood, this bull can throw one heck of a house party. She definitely earns her reputation as the "host with the most" thanks to her glamourous shindigs, which will have people talking for years to come.

You'll also notice that your Taurus friend loves indulging her whims, from massages to delicious food and the finest wine. When you're with Taurus, you can expect your senses to be richly satisfied. Her

Venusian influence means she has an appreciation of art and beauty, which is why she feels as much in her element when attending the opera as she does when relaxing at home. You can trust Taurus to thrive in her surroundings no matter where she goes—as long as she's decided that's where she wants to be, of course.

And Taurus always knows exactly what she wants. Don't let her gentle vibe fool you: if Taurus wants something badly enough, she will do whatever is necessary to get it. Everything Taurus does is deliberate; in fact, her stubbornness is often a disguise for her inner perfectionist. While this perfectionism can make it difficult to get through to her at times, you can be sure that when she offers to help you with something, like decorating your office or helping you create a budget, she'll get it done right the first time.

Written in the Stars

Your Taurus friend is a TV fanatic. Not only is chilling on the couch, binge-watching a favorite show, munching on gourmet snacks, and sipping amazing wine her ideal Sunday Funday—it's her life. Be prepared for long show marathons, and don't forget to take stretching breaks.

The Talkative Introvert: Where You'll Meet Taurus

Taurus is typically low-key. Other than going to important things, like, say, her job, it takes a lot for Taurus to leave her home. If she does leave home, she wants to be somewhere that reminds her of it and everything she loves in it, which means you'll likely meet her at a cozy café, cooking class, or even grocery store. However, if she is feeling up to it, she'll definitely wind up at the newest restaurant opening. Basically, you'll spot her anywhere there's food.

Taurus's earth element also means she has a profound respect for nature, so she enjoys participating in outdoor activities, albeit slow-moving ones, like hiking or horseback riding. All bulls also have an inner artist desperate to create something, so you can also meet one at a painting or writing class.

You'll spot Taurus by her friendly yet reserved nature. She likes to laugh and chitchat, but isn't quick to show her cards to just anyone. She enjoys meeting new people, but keeps her cool in order to protect her soft heart until her vetting process is complete.

Trustworthy and Thoughtful: How to Become Friends with Taurus

Taurus doesn't like to be rushed for anything, including friendships. She prefers to build a friendship slowly, so don't take it personally when she doesn't welcome you into her inner circle right away. Making the first move on Taurus is your best bet. Try leading with a joke to make a solid impression, as Taurus is known for having a great sense of humor—once you get it out of her. If she ribs you back, count that as a sign that she is fond of you too. Taurus also appreciates thoughtful gestures, like saving a seat for her in class or treating her to a coffee at lunch. Above everything else, Taurus wants to know that a friend is trustworthy. She doesn't take friendships lightly; when trust and depth have been developed within your connection, Taurus will see you as a lifelong friend. Making sure your actions and words match is one important way of showing your trustworthiness. If you're going to be late for her dinner party, let her know as soon as you are able. Also, open up to your Taurus friend about your deepest thoughts and feelings. This shows that you trust *her*, and that you are honest about yourself. She will be sure to reciprocate with trust and loyalty.

Shunning the Superficial: Taurus Friendship Dislikes

Superficial people are not welcome in the Taurus tribe. Taurus needs to be able to have meaningful conversations and connections with her friends; fakeness doesn't fly with this bull. While she appreciates compliments, she's suspicious of sugary accolades, as well as those who cling to her right away, and may assume such people have an illicit agenda. Flighty friends need not apply either. Taurus needs to know she can count on you through thick and thin; otherwise, the tribe has spoken.

Tolerant Temper: How Taurus Handles Conflict

Despite being symbolized by the bull, Taurus doesn't like to charge headfirst when it comes to conflict. She will do anything to keep the peace, which means she'll suppress her thoughts and feelings if necessary. This can sometimes lead to her holding a grudge. If there is a confrontation between you and Taurus, one of two scenarios will happen: either Taurus will say everything is fine when it isn't so you'll stop arguing, or she will be provoked enough to fight, in which case she will be seeing red. However, Taurus is almost always willing to forgive and forget ASAP. All she needs in return is the reassurance that your friendship means as much to you as it does to her, and you can quickly return to watching TV together. That is unless she is still holding on to that Olympic-sized grudge. In that case, the friendship could be *finito*. If you wish to avoid a grudge, you may want to treat her to her favorite snack or guilty pleasure as a peace offering.

Real and Reliable: Maintaining Your Friendship with Taurus

Because your Taurus friend is terrified of being outside of her comfort zone, it's important to respect her desire for stability. At the same time, Taurus needs a gentle push to explore new things. It's vital for her to know that change can be a good thing as it will keep her from shirking responsibility or giving up on her dreams. A little nudge in the right direction, along with a lot of love, will go a long way in expanding your Taurus pal's world, which she'll (eventually) thank you for. Encouraging and supporting her talents while helping her establish and strategize her goals is a life-changing gesture for your bull buddy.

Written in the Stars

Looking to get Taurus off that couch? When planning a trip with a Taurus friend, she will prefer destinations that are low-key yet luxurious. Since she loves to indulge her senses, especially her palate, a wine tour in Napa Valley, California, or Tuscany, Italy, would be right up her alley.

Your Taurus pal also takes loyalty and stability incredibly seriously, which is why she needs to know she can count on you during both the good times and the bad. Being a shoulder for her to lean on, sending a funny GIF on her birthday, and checking in with her regularly will mean a lot to Taurus. Extending the same compassion toward her as she bestows on you not only is meaningful, but also helps her to love and accept her imperfections. Understanding and appreciating Taurus for all she is, including—and especially—those quirks, is the greatest gift you can give.

Friendship Compatibility

Can Taurus and Aries overcome their differences? Is Pisces a good match for the grounded bull? The following section will shed light on the best compatibility matches for Taurus, as well as how she operates in a friendship with each Sun sign.

Taurus and Aries

Taurus loves routine, while Aries thrives on change. The bull is cautious, whereas the ram is impulsive. Basically (and technically, thanks to their opposing elements), it's a yin-versus-yang situation. However, differences can be refreshing. Taurus can learn to live in the moment from Aries, and Aries can learn to stop and smell the roses from Taurus. Taurus can also experience new things through Aries, while Aries will appreciate a bit of Taurus's stability. Expanding each other's horizons is the key to making this friendship last.

Taurus and Taurus

Who better to be Taurus's best friend than Taurus, right? Being friends with another bull is like being friends with a reflection of yourself—someone who completely gets you. The pros? Taurus can depend on her Taurus friend to stick by her when the going gets rough, and she can always rely on her to give the best advice. The cons? They're both so adverse to change and so stubborn that sometimes it may feel like the friendship is at a standstill. But their wine-tasting parties are like grape therapy and they LOL a lot.

Taurus and Gemini

Taurus likes to take things slowly, while Gemini knows only one speed: fast. Taurus also prefers to stick close to home, whereas Gemini loves exploring. It'll be difficult for this pair to be on the same page, but a good friendship is possible. Gemini appreciates Taurus's practical advice, while Taurus admires Gemini's clever mind. If they can see eye to eye more often than not, and not try to change each other, there's potential for this team.

Taurus and Cancer

Two homebodies unite! Cancer loves the comfort of home just as much as, if not more than, Taurus does. Together they can cook dinners, drink wine, and veg out in front of a favorite show. These two have a lot in common, establishing a foundation of stability and safety; they can tell each other anything! However, even-keeled Taurus may become irritated by Cancer's moodiness, while Cancer will disapprove of Taurus's stubbornness. Nevertheless, this friendship is meant to last.

Taurus and Leo

When Taurus is feeling sociable, there's no better person to call than Leo. They both share a passion for the finer things in life, including the trendiest cafés and the best boutiques. They also bond over their latest creative desires, and could work well together on an artistic project. Over time, the lion's boisterous and self-involved nature may annoy Taurus, while her tendency to procrastinate may frustrate Leo, who just wants to live life as much as possible.

Taurus and Virgo

Both practical and organized, these signs admire each other tremendously. Whether cooking a new recipe or planning a vacation, Taurus and Virgo work seamlessly together. They adore each other's company and appreciate that they can do a lot of "nothing" together. Virgo's honesty is music to the bull's ears, and the virgin values Taurus's loyalty. Consider these two soul mates!

Taurus and Libra

Taurus and Libra are both ruled by the planet Venus, which means they appreciate art, culture, and all things beautiful. While there is much for these two to talk about, and they can definitely get lost in a museum together, their different vibes may cause some friction. Taurus is more reserved than Libra is, who's known as one of the social butterflies of the zodiac. Libra may feel restrained by Taurus, who craves stability, while Taurus may become irritated by Libra's tendency to be a bit flaky. Patience will keep this friendship strong.

> **When Stars Align**
> Libra and Taurus enjoy the finer things in life, which means Libra can rest assured that his bull friend is the best choice to enjoy that bottle of wine with.

Taurus and Scorpio

Taurus and Scorpio are astrological opposites. While both are concerned with practical matters, Taurus is logical, whereas Scorpio is passionate. Taurus is always up-front, while Scorpio thrives on privacy. However, it's their differences that draw these two together. Taurus admires Scorpio's individuality, and Scorpio digs Taurus's sensible nature. While they might disagree on some things, their mutual love for emotional movies and wine tasting makes it easy for these two to forgive and forget.

Taurus and Sagittarius

Calm Taurus may easily be overwhelmed by Sagittarius's energetic attitude, while Sagittarius may struggle to crack the bull's reserved nature. When it comes to plans, expect some friction, as Taurus likes to stick to her routine, while Sagittarius loves a spontaneous adventure. However, these two can find things to appreciate in each other: Taurus will enjoy Sagittarius's crazy sense of humor, and Sagittarius will appreciate Taurus's loyalty. Either sign could introduce the other to a new outlook on life, which is always a good thing.

When Stars Align

In order to avoid any resentment from the bull, the archer should let her take the lead in planning a weekend excursion or special event. As someone who always knows where the best spots are, Taurus will ensure the pair never misses out on a fun location or activity.

Taurus and Capricorn

These BFFs both share a grounded, ambitious nature and have no trouble expressing their goals and dreams with each other. Even if Capricorn complains over the bull's sluggishness and Taurus gets annoyed by the sea goat's hardcore work ethic, their mutual loyalty and thoughtfulness in things like remembering birthdays and sending daily check-in texts means this friendship is filled with lots of love and will last.

Taurus and Aquarius

This is a puzzling friendship. Taurus doesn't understand why Aquarius needs to wax poetic on humanitarian issues all of the time instead of relaxing. Meanwhile, the water bearer may find the bull small-minded and a bit dull to be around. While both signs pride themselves on their integrity, Aquarius's lone wolf tendencies may alienate the friendship-oriented Taurus. Finding common ground and cooperating, rather than competing with each other, will help this friendship flourish.

Taurus and Pisces

While on the surface the earthy Taurus and dreamy Pisces might not seem like a good fit, they're actually more like peas in a pod than you may think. Flexible Pisces doesn't mind the Taurus's headstrong ways, while the bull appreciates the fish's emotional freedom. They both know a night spent at home, cooking and having kitchen dance parties together, is just as fun as (if not more than) a night out at the club. They bring out the best in each other, and love to laugh.

Friendship Planets: Venus and Jupiter

To get the full scope of a friendship, as well as how you and your friend operate individually, look at the planets of Venus and Jupiter in your charts, in addition to your Sun signs. Venus rules love and unions of all kinds, including your relationships with your friends. It reflects *how* you love others. Jupiter indicates how you *show* your love to your friends. The planet of optimism, success, and generosity, its influence nudges you to experience new things, and to be generous with others.

Venus in Taurus

The cautious and reserved nature of Venus in Taurus hides a tender heart that protects itself from drama and fake friends. Venus in Taurus prefers a friendship to unfold organically over time. But when she does open up, she is all in. Intensely loyal and always willing to lend a hand whenever needed, Venus in Taurus wants to make sure her friendships are authentic. She respects dependable people who demonstrate that they value her. She shows her love through making her friends laugh, as well as through her good-hearted deeds, which include everything from staying up late to talk out a problem with a pal, to preparing them a delicious meal. Because she loves her friends so much, she runs the risk of being possessive. It would be wise for Venus in Taurus to loosen the grip and trust that her friends love her.

Jupiter in Taurus

Grounded, generous, and patient, Jupiter in Taurus likes to make her friends feel at home. Her love for luxury and creature comforts makes her casa the perfect setting for gatherings, and she loves playing the host. She has a steady, reliable pace, which is evident by her love of tradition. She is the first to remember an anniversary, and throws one heck of a celebration. Jupiter in Taurus has an eye for beauty and finer things, and she enjoys spreading her knowledge about art collecting and interior design, as well as gifting her friends with lovely treasures from her favorite antique stores. She must learn not to overindulge her friends, as she runs the risk of "buying" her friendships. If Jupiter in Taurus stays rooted in her integrity, her tribe will appreciate her for who she is.

Chapter 3

Gemini
(May 21–June 20)

Gemini is like having two friends in one!
Symbolized by the twins, your Gemini pal
has a dual nature. On one side, Gemini is the
life of the party. As an air sign, he has a
lot to say, and will keep you laughing all
night long. On the other side, he is distracted
and brooding. But don't be discouraged:
underneath that tornado-like energy lies
a heart full of feelings.

The Talker

Gemini is ruled by Mercury, the planet of communication, including everything from texts and emails to in-person interactions. Mercury also represents intellect, and, as the planet of communication, more specifically controls how intelligence is expressed to others. It's no wonder then that your Gemini friend is smart, witty, and never seems to be at a loss for words. It can also explain why he is a sucker for a good conversation—and is never far from his phone. He is the friend who'll send you random GIFs and cat videos throughout the day. You can also blame him—or thank him—for initiating your buzzing group chat. In fact, this sign hates an awkward silence—he has to fill it with an amusing tale or a lively political debate.

Once Gemini gets talking, it's hard to keep up. He can jump from one train of thought to another in a matter of seconds. He is also amazingly skilled in making small talk with strangers, which makes him the perfect wing-person in any scenario. His inquisitive spirit often turns a conversation into an interview session because he will ask a ton of questions. But it's only because he loves learning about you! From your day at work to your latest relationship woes, he's curious because he cares.

The Wild Card

Gemini is a mutable sign, which means he was born as one season (spring) was transitioning into the next (summer). This also means that Gemini is highly adaptable, easily adjusting to a variety of situations like the social chameleon he is. This is where his twin duality comes in handy. He's the pal you can invite to either a sophisticated networking event or a family reunion barbecue, knowing he'll fit right in at both. He is also able to see both sides of any situation, which makes him a good mediator you can depend on when a problem needs to be solved.

Air signs are also considered to be the communicators of the zodiac, and Gemini, as an air sign ruled by Mercury (double whammy), does extremely well with one-on-one communication, and is particularly good at sparking fascinating debates and interesting conversations. Air signs are also constantly thinking—couple this with Gemini's inherent duality, and he is left with a mind full of swirling thoughts. It's no wonder then why he often drops one task to do another before the first is finished (like suddenly forgetting to plan your ski trip because he needs to buy cat food).

This unpredictability is also evidenced in his fashion sense. Whether it's dyeing his hair pink or wearing haute couture, the twin definitely likes to make a statement with his image. To Gemini, his sense of style helps express who he is, and in having dual personalities, anything goes with him. He likes mixing things up, from basics to bold prints, and loves keeping people guessing as to what he'll wear next.

Gemini Quirks: The Know-It-All Twin

Your Gemini friend is supersmart. You know it, and
(somewhat irritatingly) so does he. He also won't hold
back with his knowledge, relaying any compliment
or criticism that comes to mind. For the most part,
however, the twin's brashness comes from a sense of
protection. Whether or not you want to hear it, you
probably need to know what Gemini has to say—and
he will say it. It's not just because he's right (which he
probably is), but it's also because he is skilled at dispensing advice and intuitively knowing when a friend
is in need.

However, this wealth of knowledge can lead to a
false sense of leadership, because Gemini believes
being a good leader means knowing more than others. Suffice to say, your Gemini pal always has to be
right. Even when he is wrong, he is right. If you don't
want to risk an epic fight, it is better to let go of the

subject (even if you know you are right) so you can move on.

Gossip and a Gargantuan Spirit

Because Gemini has the potential to win a congeniality contest, he attracts a lot of admirers. His adaptability and enthusiasm make it easy for him to move between social circles with ease, winning new friends with his witty sense of humor, joie de vivre, and intelligence. This also means he is privy to a lot of info from many different people, which can lead to accusations of him stirring the pot. While he may not mean to cause trouble, he does have a tendency to gossip and overshare, which can cause some people to rethink opening up to him. However, your twin friend is one of the most compassionate people around, so if he spills the tea, it's only because his mouth got ahead of his thoughts. Most of the time, what you might consider gossip, Gemini sees as just an interesting piece of information worth sharing.

Gemini's electric spirit also means he hates being bored. He likes to fill his weekends with museum visits and spontaneous road trips so he can avoid staying still at all costs. From attending a carnival to camping, as long as it keeps his mind stimulated and his spirit fulfilled, happy-go-lucky Gemini is content to do just about anything. If you ever find yourself bored, text your Gemini friend. He will find a way to keep you both occupied. On the flip side, with Gemini's constant need for change and entertainment, friends might become drained or frustrated with Gemini's inability to sit still. His flightiness can also make him unreliable. One minute he is in town, and the next minute he is halfway across the country on a new adventure.

Class Clown: Where You'll Meet Gemini

Fun-loving and eager to try new things, Gemini can be found anywhere that keeps his mind stimulated. From trivia matches to a writing class, Gemini is in his element when he is able to attain new knowledge while showing off his clever mind. As an intellectual who doesn't like routines, he tends to hate the gym, but is attracted to adventure sports, particularly those related to the sky (thanks to his air element), so don't be surprised if you meet Gemini while paragliding or skydiving.

Since he adores solving puzzles, the twin is also equally happy to be curled up on a couch at a café tackling a crossword or sudoku puzzle. You'll instantly recognize Gemini by his big laugh, mischievous vibe, and unique fashion sense. No matter where you meet Gemini, you can be sure he'll be front and center, eagerly asking questions and displaying his smarts while simultaneously making everyone LOL.

Enticing and Engaging: How to Become Friends with Gemini

Gemini is like a cat: he is a fickle creature, but if you
entice him with something intriguing, you'll get his
attention. For Gemini, this might be a funny remark
or an invitation to a contemporary art exhibit. When
approaching the twin, keep in mind that he responds
to lightness, compliments, and friendly banter. This
air sign thrives when topics of conversation are of the
watercooler variety—meaning they are airy and non-
confrontational. Any celebrity gossip is welcome too.
He isn't comfortable with deep, emotional discussions,
especially not when he is just getting to know you.
Do remember also that once Gemini starts talking, he
won't stop. Accepting his need to monopolize a tête-à-
tête will help your friendship thrive. Prove yourself a
worthy conversationalist, and you've found yourself a
friend in Gemini.

Slow and Stagnant: Gemini Friendship Dislikes

Gemini can become impatient and dismissive when someone isn't as clever or knowledgeable as he is. He doesn't like to repeat himself either, so if you didn't catch what came spurting out of his mouth a moment ago, he's already moved on to the next thing. Gemini also needs a friend who can keep up with him in all other avenues of his life. He hates routine and monotony, so the ideal ally likes freedom and change as much as he does. If you're up for a spur-of-a-moment road trip one weekend, or want to join in on an impromptu rally for a cause, you're a perfect match for Gemini. On the other hand, try pinning him down and you won't see him for his dust.

Avoidance or Assault: How Gemini Handles Conflict

Symbolized by the twins, it is not surprising that Gemini handles conflict in one of two very different ways.

Option A has Gemini avoiding conflict at all costs, especially if he deems a situation pointless and not worth his time. He'll simply stay out of it, and continue on with his life. Being the intellectual he is, if an argument is too dull, he'll yawn and move on.

Option B unleashes Gemini's angry Hulk side. You'll tend to see this side if you've insulted Gemini's intelligence, or accused him of being wrong (Gemini never thinks he's wrong). In this version, Gemini isn't afraid to stand up for himself, and he'll unleash his anger amidst a flurry of cutting words, which will certainly leave you wounded. Since a Gemini struggles to admit when he is wrong, it can be difficult to make amends after this kind of conflict. Getting him to accept his erroneous behavior is nearly impossible. So what's the best way to deal with an angry Gemini? Don't engage with him. Simply say what you need to say once, and then walk away. Pulling the plug on an argument will diffuse Gemini's anger, allowing him the space to cool down and move on.

Communication and a Safe Space: Maintaining Your Friendship with Gemini

Your Gemini friend has a reputation for saying things off the cuff, which can sometimes lead to hurt feelings. During these instances, it's important to remember that the twin operates from a cerebral plane: he thinks first, feels second. Oftentimes when he speaks out of turn, he doesn't realize the emotional implications of his words. Try to not take these moments personally. If possible, shrug it off and trust that Gemini doesn't mean to offend you. However, if it is something that you can't ignore, communicate with him. He appreciates honest and clear communication, and he is quick to learn from his mistakes.

Because your twin pal's mind is akin to a whirlwind, he often forgets appointments or events, and can have trouble finishing a task. Keeping him accountable will help him follow through—he might even show up to your birthday early this year.

And speaking of showing up (or in this case not showing up), your Gemini friend's restless nature means he is constantly changing things up and meeting new friends. This is why there may be days, weeks, or even months when you don't hear from him. Understand that he is just caught up with the latest new thing—he doesn't mean to go MIA on you. In order to keep yourself from taking this personally, it's key that you maintain interests and friends outside of your friendship with Gemini. Remember that your Gemini friend does care about you and will come back around when he's ready.

Gemini also has difficulty with vulnerability. He prefers to keep interactions entertaining and fun, and will brush aside anything that might be troubling him. Don't let his outward appearance fool you: he needs to talk about his feelings sometimes too. Let your twin friend know that your friendship is a safe space for him to share and process whatever is weighing on him. He might not take you up on the offer right away, but the gesture will mean the world to him.

Friendship Compatibility

What is it exactly that makes two Geminis better than one? How might Gemini and his Cancer friend overcome their differences? In the following section, you will discover Gemini's compatibility matches, as well as how he operates in a friendship with each sign.

Gemini and Aries

This is an exciting combination because both signs prefer to be out of the house. Their mutual high energy and curiosity make these two ideal traveling companions. From discovering new outdoor activities to taking the mic at a karaoke night, there's never a dull moment in this friendship. While they might butt heads over who's right and who's wrong, learning to compromise will allow this beautiful friendship to flourish.

When Stars Align

Both Gemini and Aries love talking. If Aries needs someone to bounce ideas off of, or wants to discuss the latest headlines, he shouldn't hesitate to text the twin.

Gemini and Taurus

Taurus craves stability, while Gemini prefers to mix things up. Disagreements over what to do on a Friday night are inevitable, as well as many differences of opinion. However, Gemini likes the comfort that Taurus provides, while Taurus finds Gemini's lively spirit contagious. If they can each see how the other person is the missing link in their life, these two will learn to live harmoniously together—it's a friendship that gets better with age.

When Stars Align

Taurus is a calming voice of reason for the chaotic, impulsive Gemini. When a conflict arises, Taurus should remain levelheaded and give Gemini space, as getting angry will just rile him up even more.

Gemini and Gemini

Rowdiness alert. Put these two twins together, and you get a duo crazier than a bag of cats. The two Geminis feed off each other, constantly challenging and trying to outdo the other in every adventure. It may be hard for anyone to get a word in edgewise, and these friends might compete with each other more than complete each other, but they feel most like themselves when they're side by side, and are grateful for the freedom this connection offers.

Gemini and Cancer

Cancer is a homebody who values emotional support and a stable foundation. Gemini is the complete opposite, thriving on change and often refusing to go deep with his emotions. Their differences will be hard to overlook at times, but each will enjoy the other's company. Cancer loves Gemini's exciting stories, while Gemini appreciates Cancer's tenderness. This friendship can last if both parties focus on their fondness for each other, rather than their differences.

Gemini and Leo

These two friends love to laugh together. They both see life through the same optimistic lens, and always manage to have a good time no matter what they're doing. They value each other's playful spirit, and their mutual passion for creativity is an endless source of fun and mental stimulation. There are few arguments because Gemini doesn't mind Leo taking center stage. Talking and laughing into the late hours is one of the highlights of this friendship.

Gemini and Virgo

Gemini and Virgo are both ruled by Mercury, which makes communication the basis of their friendship. They enjoy engaging with each other in intellectual conversations on current events and literature, and because they both like to read so much, they could even start their own book club. However, Virgo may feel that

Gemini is immature and callous at times, while Gemini may find Virgo too stiff and parental.

Gemini and Libra

This is an easy connection that feels meant to be. Both Gemini and Libra love going out and socializing, and since each understands the other's need for more friends and experiences, they seldom get jealous or feel left out. Making decisions is hard between these two, as Gemini is constantly changing his mind and Libra never knows what choice to make. However, they are perfectly content to do anything as long as they're together, which is the marking of true BFFs.

Gemini and Scorpio

Gemini and Scorpio may wonder why they're friends, and it's not hard to see why they might wonder. Each sign can be stubborn and moody, and because they are both so private with their emotions, they often feel like they don't really know each other—and they may not. Their fights can be explosive, with neither person wanting to admit when they are wrong. It will take growth on both sides to make this friendship work.

Gemini and Sagittarius

These two friends most likely met abroad, as they share a deep sense of adventure. Because they also both love meeting new people and being spontaneous, there's never a dull moment between them. However, Gemini and Sagittarius are astrological opposites, meaning they can tire of each other quickly. Gemini may find Sagittarius too bossy, while Sagittarius thinks Gemini can be too wishy-washy. They may consider centering their hangouts around travel.

Gemini and Capricorn

Opposites attract when Gemini and Capricorn come together. Gemini can help serious Capricorn live more in the moment, while Capricorn can guide the flaky Gemini in making his long-term goals a reality. However, both signs are stubborn and hate to lose, which can result in disagreements, and their disparate perspectives on life might stifle their connection. If they can be patient with each other and celebrate their differences, this will be a lasting friendship.

Gemini and Aquarius

These two independent signs are made for each other. Creative and intellectual, Gemini and Aquarius love getting into lively debates with each other and have fun wandering museums, learning and exploring together. While the water bearer's intense focus might be too, well, intense at times for the flighty twin, these friends understand each other very well, and they appreciate each other's unconventional lifestyle.

Gemini and Pisces

While this pairing has the potential to balance each other out well, it also has a few challenges. Gemini might think Pisces is too sensitive, while Pisces will want a deeper emotional connection to Gemini than he is ready to offer. Additionally, Gemini's need to go out and try new things may clash with the downtime that Pisces craves. If able to reconcile their differences, Gemini can open up Pisces's world and Pisces can help Gemini get in touch with his feelings.

Friendship Planets: Venus and Jupiter

Considering the locations of Venus and Jupiter in both your friend's and your charts, in addition to your Sun signs, can help you gain a better understanding of your friend and your friendship. The sensual planet Venus rules love and unions of all kinds, including friendships. It indicates *how* you love. Jupiter, meanwhile, reflects how you *show* your love to your friends. The planet of optimism, success, and generosity, it encourages you to experience new things in life, and to be generous with others.

Venus in Gemini

Venus in Gemini has no trouble winning over friends with his quick wit, charm, and endless source of knowledge. He's always up for a good time, and enjoys engaging others in clever conversation and making them laugh. His friendships thrive on activity and talking about the latest news, from headlines to celebrity gossip, into the wee hours of the night. Heavy emotions feel too stifling for Venus in Gemini, so he prefers to keep his connections light, which explains why he stays busy and has many circles of friends. This difficulty with emotions may make it difficult for him to get close to people at times, but while his detachment might alienate some, friends are drawn to his childlike fun.

Jupiter in Gemini

Jupiter in Gemini is naturally adventurous. He loves inspiring his friends to chase after new experiences and opportunities. Gifted with a sharp mind, he dazzles people with fascinating facts and figures, little-known tidbits, and crazy anecdotes. Because Jupiter influences writers and Gemini is big on communication, Jupiter in Gemini likes to share his creative gifts with his friends, which might include writing long emails or texts as a means of making up for lost time, or teaming up with them on artistic endeavors. It's important for Jupiter in Gemini to watch out for information overload, allowing his friends the space to figure things out for themselves and giving them a moment to digest his frantic energy.

Chapter 4

Cancer
(June 21–July 22)

Ruled by the Moon, which represents feelings and your deepest needs, Cancer feels the tides of her emotions more intensely than most. And like the Moon, her mood constantly shifts—from empathetic one minute to snappy the next (no wonder her symbol is the crab). Underneath a hard exterior lies a mushy center that longs to feel connected. You just have to crack it open first.

The Mama (or Papa) Bear

If one were to designate an individual sign as the den mother (or father) of the zodiac, it would be Cancer. Reminiscent of her planetary ruler, the Moon, Cancer is both a nurturer and protector, especially when it comes to those closest to her. And like a parental figure, Cancer will do whatever she can to make sure her friends are being taken care of. While Cancer's astrological opposite Capricorn takes on the traditional patriarchal role with rules and structure, Cancer is all about maternal instinct.

As a water sign, Cancer is intuitive and sensitive, and is keenly tuned in to the emotions of others (much like a mother figure). She wants to know what's going on in your world 24/7. If something's bugging you, she won't stop asking about it until you tell her who or what's responsible for hurting you. In return, she'll offer you sympathy and the soundest advice—and maybe a warrant for the perpetrator's arrest. Furthermore, she will do whatever it takes to keep the peace between loved ones, as she hates to see any of her "children" fighting. For example, she might arrange a meeting in which she'll act as mediator to help you and another friend talk things out. She might also use her keen intuition and empathy to provide insight into your situation in the hopes of finding a resolution.

Cancer is also a cardinal sign (meaning she was born at the beginning of the summer season), which denotes initiation and action. She sees it as her job to plan get-togethers, like dinners and picnics, and is happiest when she is running the show. She likes to know that she is putting her best foot forward in all situations, so that no matter what happens, she feels she did her very best. Which explains why her parties are always top-notch, and why she has exceptional follow-through when it comes to creative projects or high school reunions.

The Homebody

As a nurturing water sign, it's Cancer's mission to help her friends feel at home whenever they're in her company. And if Cancer has her way, friends will want to spend their time at her home. Symbolized by the crab, she is very comfortable staying within her shell, and it takes a lot for her to leave it. When given the choice to stay in or go out, Cancer will always opt to stay in—home is her safe haven.

> **Written in the Stars**
> When planning a vacation with homebody Cancer, keep in mind her desire to feel comfortable. She will enjoy a cozy inn or bed-and-breakfast, preferably near water (her astrological element); take her to one in Cape Cod, Massachusetts, or Newport, Rhode Island.

Not surprisingly, Cancer knows how to decorate an abode, and her friends prefer to hang out at her casa anyway because it's beautifully furnished and so very tidy. Another bonus? Cancer tends to be a great cook! When Cancer cooks, she cooks with love, so she doesn't mind whipping up delicious meals for her friends. Cancer also believes "the more, the merrier" when it comes to entertaining (so long as she's vetted the guests beforehand), so her parties are certainly memorable.

Being a homebody also means that your Cancer friend often retreats into her shell to chill out, and needs regular bouts of alone time in order to recharge. If you encroach upon her territory during one of her private moods, you'll certainly get a dose of the crabbiness that she can be known for—no wonder her astrological symbol is the crab.

Written in the Stars

Getting outside every once in a while is healthy for Cancer, particularly since she can tend to stay indoors for too long, sometimes getting a bit too lost in the past or falling victim to lethargy. Because Cancer is a water sign, she has a natural connection to water, so anything water-related, including hitting the beach, taking a dip in a pool, or even sailing, will interest her.

Cancer Quirks: The Moody Crab

One thing's clear: the crab's moodiness always keeps you guessing. In one instant, she is compassionate and funny (Cancer has a fantastic sense of humor), then in another, she can be withdrawn and even sullen. There are a couple of reasons for this. First, her sensitive nature can make it difficult for her to process and deal with her emotions. Feeling so much all the time tires your crab friend, which in turn can make her more touchy.

Second, Cancer often believes she has something to prove. It's normal for her to feel like she is undervalued, despite the fact that she works really hard at everything she does. Deep down, Cancer may see the rest of the world as against her. Because of this, she often seeks approval from others, including her friends. The rub is that she actually resents seeking this validation, because she knows that she is just as intelligent and industrious as everyone else—if not more so; however, no matter how hard she tries in everything, she still requires recognition for her hard work. The upside to this need is that Cancer is instilled with an impressive tenacity as a result. When she goes after something, she goes all out, with a full heart. Chances are your most memorable nights out and delicious home-cooked meals are all thanks to your crab friend.

What may be most surprising about Cancer, however, is her unwillingness to share her emotions with others. Friends may flock to her with their troubles, but Cancer is tight-lipped about her own. Much like her astrological symbol, she has a protective outer shell that is hard to penetrate. While she has no problem with offering you advice and support for your issues, she doesn't want to reveal or burden you with her own, whether it be out of self-preservation, or her desire to ensure your comfort. It's not personal; it's just how she's built.

Soothsaying and Sentimentality

Cancer's high emotional intelligence is borderline psychic; your crab friend can walk into a room and easily read the mood. While her thick shell provides her with quite the poker face, she always knows what's up, and, most importantly, who to approach. This gut instinct is why she is so adept at providing insight into your latest turmoil, and it's what helps inform her reasoning when she offers her advice. It's her "Spidey sense," and it's seldom wrong. Her deep-rooted maternal nature kicks in whenever her friends are in need of advice, and she doesn't hesitate to share her wisdom, as her loved ones are the most important thing to her. After all, when you're as devoted to family as Cancer is, being sentimental comes with the deal.

Cancer is a sucker for nostalgia. You'll find that she has a keen recollection, and often references past people, relationships, and situations; she may say, "Remember when…?" a lot. While it's sweet that Cancer still has a shoebox under her bed full of mementoes, her refusal to let go of the past can also be harmful at times. She is the friend who'll desperately hold on to a relationship no matter how toxic it is, insisting she can still be friends with an ex or someone who's wronged her. This is also partly due to the fact that she often romanticizes the past, and goes for an occasional walk down memory lane as an escape from reality. Sometimes her idolization of "what was" is also rooted in her dependency on her friends. Because when Cancer says that you're friends for life, she quite literally means it.

The Observer: Where You'll Meet Cancer

Encountering Cancer outside of her home is like spotting a unicorn. It rarely happens outside of work, or other places of necessity like the grocery store. Her affinity for home means she prefers indoor activities, especially those related to domesticity. She is most likely to show up at a cooking, carpentry, or sewing class. Because Cancer also has a rich imagination and a natural creative instinct, she is drawn to the arts, and could very well be sitting in front of you at a poetry reading or a painting class. Her empathetic nature, as well as her need to get out of her own head, will also lead her to volunteer at organizations close to her heart, like a children's hospital or food bank.

Cancer is a natural observer, and will get a feel for the room before talking to anyone. She is an intrinsically cautious person, and is often hard to read, especially for those who don't know her very well. However, she does have an easygoing vibe that makes her quick to laugh and smile, which puts most people at ease upon meeting her.

Patience and Persistence: How to Become Friends with Cancer

Cancer is naturally introverted, so chances are you will have to initiate the approach. Don't be surprised when, upon your opening handshake, Cancer appears cautious toward you. She's so busy managing her feelings and sizing you up, while also trying to come across as likeable, that it can be a little overwhelming for her. To help break the ice, Cancer always welcomes a compliment. A stamp of approval is music to her ears, which will help her slowly yet surely come out of her shell. Just make sure you're being authentic, as the crab can smell a phony a mile away.

Because she is so choosy with whom she welcomes into her tribe, she might not take you up on your lunch invitation the first time. Or even the second time. However, the third time may be the charm. If you remain persistent, she'll start to take your offer of friendship seriously.

Ungrateful and Disloyal: Cancer Friendship Dislikes

When it comes to her friendships, Cancer is extremely generous with her time, wisdom, clothing, cooking skills—pretty much anything and everything. She gives from her heart and doesn't expect anything in return. However, she doesn't like her generosity to be taken for granted. She gives her friendships her all, so her biggest fear is being taken for a sucker. Since her friendships are her everything, Cancer also wants her friends to extend the same loyalty. If a crab believes you're being disingenuous and questions your allegiance, you're almost "dead" to her. *Almost*—because Cancer doesn't like to end a friendship. If you're not "dead" to her in this case, you're certainly demoted.

The Big Sulk: How Cancer Handles Conflict

Cancer is passive aggressive when it comes to conflict. Typically, she avoids confrontation like the plague. A crab would much rather suppress her feelings, which she's naturally prone to do anyway, and act out in subversive ways, than confront an issue. If someone attacks her, her response is to sulk or go MIA. If you want to get to the bottom of your conflict with Cancer, you'll have to provoke it out of her. Luckily, this isn't too difficult to do, since Cancer hates being in a fight with a friend. She can't live with the notion that she might have hurt her friend's feelings, and is more ashamed of committing such an act than anything else. This is why it's so easy for her to dissolve into a puddle of tears at the first hint of a fight. Really, Cancer doesn't even care whose fault it is—she just wants to kiss and make up as quickly as possible. However, beware: underneath Cancer's forgiving nature is someone who'll quietly hold a grudge if she believes you broke an oath.

Safety and Security: Maintaining Your Friendship with Cancer

Let's be honest: Cancer's crabby mood might be frustrating to endure at times. While it's easy, and certainly understandable, to become irritated with her flip-floppy emotions, it's important to understand that it's simply her nature. Cancer's moodiness isn't necessarily a reflection on you or how she feels about your friendship. You can skip out on numerous squabbles with your Cancer friend by accepting this as part of who she is, while also giving her the space to digest her emotions.

While your Cancer friend comes across as confident in her relationships, she lives in constant fear of being rejected and abandoned, which is especially sad considering how skilled she is at helping you to feel loved and secure. That's why it's imperative to check in with your crab pal regularly and let her know how much you appreciate her friendship. Whether it's surprising her with a video chat catch-up session or a take-out pizza at her place, regular affirmation goes a long way.

Giving your Cancer friend a safe space to express herself and her emotions is another amazing gift you can give to her. Prove to her, both through your words and your actions, that you're a trustworthy friend who wants to be her sounding board as much as she is for you, and that she can trust you with her innermost secrets. Despite her hard shell, a crab does yearn for the connection that vulnerability creates. While she might not initially take you up on your offer, letting her know she can safely share these things with you will mean the world to her.

Friendship Compatibility

What is behind the close bond between Cancer and Taurus? How might the sensitivities of Cancer and Leo work together to create a lasting friendship? The following section details each of Cancer's compatibility matches, as well as how she operates in friendships with signs who may not be included in her top matches.

Cancer and Aries

Cancer's sensitivity and protectiveness might be too much for Aries, who wants a partner in crime—not a parent. Additionally, the crab might think the ram's need for independence and autonomy is a little selfish and indifferent. However, these two do have things in common: they both make great leaders, and they can help inspire each other to achieve their dreams.

Focusing on their strengths while admiring each other's differences will make this friendship a winner.

Cancer and Taurus

These two homebodies share a deep love for movie nights in—and deep-dish pizza. They also both take pleasure in security and spending time with friends and family. Enjoying the simple things in life, like good food and wine, hiking, and deep talks, cements their kinship. While the bull might think the crab is too moody at times, and the crab might get frustrated with the bull's lethargy, these two make a wonderful pair.

Cancer and Gemini

Gemini doesn't understand why Cancer cares so much about everything, while Cancer feels that Gemini doesn't care *enough*. While the crab may get annoyed at how distracted the twin can be, and the twin dislikes the crab's attachment to the past, this can be a powerful friendship if given a chance. Gemini can add a much-needed dosage of fun and spontaneity to Cancer's life, while Cancer's thoughtfulness will warm Gemini in a way he didn't realize he needed. There's a lot these two can learn from each other.

Cancer and Cancer

Two Cancers = soul mates. No other sign understands the feels that Cancer experiences, and no one else appreciates her weird sense of humor in the same way either. Thanks to their powerful intuition, it's like they're reading each other's minds (which may be the case). While their mutual moodiness could make things tricky at times, they each understand the importance of giving the other space.

Cancer and Leo

These two are sensitive, but for different reasons. Cancer can be touchy because of her intense feelings, while Leo's ego can cause him to be easily offended. Because these two are effectively wounded by criticism, they constantly need to be validated, which can be exhausting for both parties. While this friendship may be difficult at times, there is a lot of love here. The lion appreciates the crab's tenderness, and the crab admires the lion's playful attitude. Plus, they'll both love Cancer's gourmet cooking.

Cancer and Virgo

Both Cancer and Virgo carefully curate their friends, which means if they decide to become friends with each other, there is a good reason for it. Cancer appreciates Virgo's thoughtful diligence, including how she always surprises her with the perfect gift. Meanwhile, Virgo admires Cancer's mothering, because the virgin often neglects her own needs. However, Virgo's nitpicking and Cancer's emotional outbursts can cause conflict, so communication will be key.

Cancer and Libra

Relationships are extremely important to both of these signs, and they love to prioritize the special people in their lives. However, when Libra's logic comes up against Cancer's emotions, differences will arise. Cancer wants emotional security and cozy nights in, whereas Libra wants creative stimulation and prefers to socialize. But seeing as they both dread conflict, they'll end up compromising and sweeping their problems under the carpet—which can be bad *or* good for the friendship's future.

Cancer and Scorpio

There are more moods than a mood ring in this combo, which means things are bound to get intense. However, both signs can also count on deep discussions, emotional understanding, and a meaningful connection that seems like it's meant to be. The crab understands the scorpion's weird passions like no other, and the scorpion admires the crab's dedication to home and hearth. While Scorpio doesn't like it when Cancer sulks, and Cancer finds Scorpio a little harsh at times, they will learn to live with each other's quirks because no one else accepts them so unconditionally.

Cancer and Sagittarius

Cancer needs someone to stick by her through thick and thin, and Sagittarius can't guarantee where he'll be tomorrow. Suffice to say the uncertainty of Sagittarius's life and attitude makes Cancer insecure, while

Sagittarius may feel stifled by Cancer's neediness. Sagittarius wants to travel the world and Cancer wants to stick close to home, which will inevitably be a sticking point in the friendship. While their differences can complement each other, they'll both need patience to make this friendship a bull's-eye.

Cancer and Capricorn

These two are astrological opposites, but this is the secret ingredient to their winning friendship "recipe." The crab's emotional intelligence helps the sea goat to see the bigger picture of her goals, while the sea goat's practicality gives more grounding to the crab's side hustle dreams. Sometimes Capricorn will think Cancer too moody, while Cancer will feel Capricorn is too stoic, but they can overlook these flaws because they truly enjoy each other's company.

When Stars Align
These signs don't make the best of roommates. Chances are they'll fight over cleanliness and noise levels. Like many great friendships, this bond requires enough personal space to avoid each being at the other's throat.

Cancer and Aquarius

Opposites don't really attract with this pairing. Cancer is a traditionalist, while Aquarius is anything but. The crab loves the comfort of home, while the water bearer is all about going out into the world. Cancer also relies on the stability and loyalty of her friends, while Aquarius doesn't need a lot of devotion from his relationships. While both enjoy water activities, it will take an acceptance of each other's differences to keep this friendship afloat.

When Stars Align

It's important for Aquarius to check in with Cancer regularly. Otherwise, the sensitive crab will take his aloofness personally and might check out of the friendship.

Cancer and Pisces

Get out the tissues because this is one friendship that's all about the feels. Through heartbreak, laughter, and countless nights watching rom-com movies, Cancer and Pisces embody #friendshipgoals. Their emotional bond is intuitive, which means they profoundly understand each other. Pisces helps Cancer feel safe in leaving her shell for a while, and Cancer supports Pisces's wildest dreams. While this bond can get so intense that it becomes a little draining—they shouldn't spend *all* of their time together—Cancer and Pisces have a connection that's like no other.

Friendship Planets: Venus and Jupiter

Looking at where Venus and Jupiter are in your friend's and your charts can further help you understand that friend and your relationship with them. The sensual planet Venus rules love and unions of all kinds, including friendships. Its location in your birth chart indicates *how* you love. Jupiter, meanwhile, is the planet of optimism, success, and generosity, and indicates how you *show* your love to those close to you.

Venus in Cancer

Despite an exterior shell of caution and self-protection, Venus in Cancer has a sensitive soul, which is why friendships are so important to her. She loves being in the company of people she cares for. However, since friendships matter so much to her, Venus in Cancer needs the assurance that her friends value and love her in return. As a result, she'll hang back until a friend proves their loyalty to her. Once she does feel secure, there's no holding back: she will go all out for her friends. Venus in Cancer lives for demonstrating just how much her loved ones mean to her, like throwing huge celebrations for birthdays and milestones, and surprising them with homemade gifts. Sentimental, she will hold on to friendships for years and years—even long after they may have reached their expiration date. It's essential for her to learn to let go of what is no longer serving her, as well as to take the time to create a safe space for her feelings so she is able to sift and sort through them.

Jupiter in Cancer

Jupiter in Cancer approaches her friendships with an emotional awareness that's evident in everything she does. She takes the time to nourish her friendships, whether that means pursuing creative collaborative projects, cooking up delicious dinners, or catching up through deep discussions. Most likely to help a friend in need, Jupiter in Cancer always provides a safe haven in which her friends are free to share their innermost secrets and fears.

She also takes great pride in her home, and might even pride herself on her DIY skills, so she'll eagerly help a friend redecorate or reorganize their abode. She often feels like she has more than she needs, so she is happy to pass on old books and clothing to her friends as well. However, her intense feelings and need for closeness could result in emotional overload for her pals, so she should make sure she doesn't become too clingy or intrusive in their lives.

Chapter 5

Leo

(July 23–August 22)

"Strike a pose" is a phrase quite fitting of Leo. Ruled by the Sun, Leo is a natural performer whose exuberant energy is quite contagious. When in the company of Leo, you can't help but be struck by his warmth. If you can live with his mighty roar, he'll welcome you into his pride with open arms.

The Pleasure-Seeker

Much like his ruling planet, the Sun, which spreads light throughout the planetary system and is the prime source of all energy, Leo is vivacious, fun-loving, and a bit self-indulgent. He expects to be the center of attention (just like his planetary ruler) and often is. Vibrant and grandiose, Leo is also a fire sign, which makes him almost doubly enthusiastic for a life well lived. He is all about pleasure, creativity, and expression. In other words, he is only interested in doing the things that make his heart sing, which include anything from creative projects to emotional outlets. He knows that life is more than adhering to a nine-to-five, five days a week routine. That's why your Leo pal will invite you to the latest Broadway musical in the middle of the afternoon, or talk you out of staying late at work so you can hit up the latest action flick together.

Being the epicurean sign that he is, it's safe to say that if Leo considers you a friend, then it is because you add pleasure to his life. He not only loves spending time with you, but he also finds your emotional connection enriching and inspiring. Your friendship feels good to him.

Written in the Stars
If traveling with your Leo friend, keep in mind that the lion is all about that luxe life. He wants to travel to the most glam destinations and stay in only the poshest of hotels. Don't be surprised when he suggests L.A., Paris, or Ibiza.

The Giver

Leo is a fixed sign, which means he was born at the height of a season (summer). As a fixed sign, he is bestowed with a powerful sense of purpose, which explains why Leo is on a lifelong mission to live his best life and be his best self. A key part of that mission also includes helping out his loved ones in any way he can. Blessed with a heart of gold, Leo is truly one of the kindest friends you'll have. Being a fixed sign also means he is a reliable friend who enjoys taking care of you, and will dote on you, bringing you chicken soup when you're sick or sending you impromptu text messages of love and encouragement just because. He is always excited to hear about your biggest dreams, and will help you make them happen. Your achievements are his achievements; he is the friend who's more excited for your wedding, job promotion, or new car than even you are.

You can trust your lion friend to surprise you with the best gifts ever (Leo is known for being an excellent gift giver) or pick up the tab at lunch. And if he can't treat you with something for one reason or another, then he'll probably give you the shirt off his back—that's how darn thoughtful he can be. While Leo certainly doesn't mind attention for his big heart (his ego can't help it), that's not why he does the incredible things he does. He does them because it's simply how he is built. Just how generous can he be? Well, let's put it this way: as much as your lion pal loves the spotlight (and he does), he has no issue sharing the stage with you. He is excited to see you shine too (just not so bright that you outshine him, because, well, he is ruled by the Sun, after all).

Leo Quirks: The Loyal Lion

Once you've made it behind his velvet ropes of friendship, there's one thing you'll never have to question about your Leo friend: his loyalty. Like his astrological symbol, the lion, Leo is one of the most loyal signs of the zodiac, which means you can expect your friendship to last a lifetime. He will protect you as fiercely as a mother lion protects her cubs; if someone upsets one of his own, they should be prepared to deal with Leo's intimidating growl.

As a result of his protectiveness, your Leo friend can be very territorial of his tribe members. He can easily become jealous of those with whom he has to share your attention—including lovers and other friends—and he has no qualms with expressing his disapproval of this scenario. This can feel a bit ironic, since you yourself will need to share his attentions with a large social circle. After all, thanks to his dazzling personality and innate love for people, Leo is adept at meeting and making friends wherever he goes. While you might feel tempted to point out this double standard to your lion friend, you may want to reconsider: Leo can be indignant when he feels he's been wronged, and won't hesitate to pout. Luckily, while his ever-growing tribe means his calendar is usually full, he won't hesitate to extend an invitation for you to join in the fun.

Royal Blood and Running the Show

The lion is the monarch: the king (or queen) of the jungle—and Leo knows this with every fiber of his soul. Why else would he walk into any room like he owns it (and he does)? Your lion friend is, to say the least, confident. He believes he is the best, and therefore deserves the best that life has to offer. And as fixed sign (which is linked to inflexibility), he is pretty stubborn about this tenet. If there's something Leo wants, he'll chase after it with a concentrated focus like no other. Even if you disagree with what Leo is pursuing, once a goal is within his crosshairs, he won't flinch. He wants that crown.

Leo's intense ambition, coupled with his desire for nothing short of excellence, is why he often insists on running the show. After all, he does rule the kingdom—or at least tries to. From dinner parties to work projects to home renovations, Leo will take charge, making sure every detail is done to his liking (and he has quite high standards). Not surprisingly, this meticulousness and extreme self-assuredness can make it difficult for people to collaborate with him. If you dare disagree with him, you'll probably encounter his infamous tantrum; Leo is a temperamental creature, especially when his ego has been bruised. If you choose not to work with him, he'll work without you—the show must go on, after all.

And speaking of shows, an inherent knack for theatrics is a trademark of your Leo friend. He is often gifted in storytelling, and knows how to garner attention with just about anything he says. Leo can make pushing a cart through the grocery store sound like a high-speed car chase. Just like his planetary ruler, Leo truly is the brightest star.

Leo enjoys playing his star role in every way, including how he presents himself to the world. There is no doubt your lion pal loves spending his time and money on pampering, ensuring that his nails are neat and his hair is always perfectly coiffed. He is always impeccably dressed as well. If you can't afford a personal stylist, you can definitely learn a lot about fashion and grooming from your Leo buddy, and he'll be happy to share his tips with you. The downside of his passion for glitz and glamour? If there isn't drama in his world, Leo will certainly create it. Whether it's by embellishing an incident or spilling the tea about others, Leo lives for excitement.

Written in the Stars

Being the big vamp that he is, anywhere there is a stage to perform on is where Leo wants to be. Whether it's cutting a rug on the dance floor or doing stand-up, your Leo friend enjoys himself the most whenever he is in the limelight. Take a seat and cheer him on.

The Performer: Where You'll Meet Leo

Leo loves to be where the people are. Interacting with others feeds his energy and provides him with an outlet to show off his skills (or latest pair of shoes). With his strong personality and urge to shine, Leo can be found virtually anywhere there are eyes to see him. Therefore, anything to do with the performing arts, from dancing to poetry to singing, is a natural fit for him. Leo also has an abundance of energy, which he loves to burn off in high-intensity activities like running, surfing, and ice-skating. His need to make a mark in his lifetime will often lead him to take up philanthropic work as well.

But regardless of where you go, you won't have to look very hard to recognize Leo. He's the one who is taking the mic, energizing and charming the crowd. But while some may be inclined to write him off as a show-off, chances are his sunny personality will win you over.

Bold and Bubbly: How to Become Friends with Leo

More than likely Leo will approach you first because of his desire to make friends with everyone. But if you do make your way to Leo first, don't be afraid to speak up. Leo isn't hard to please; however, he does appreciate his ego being stroked. Dish out a genuine compliment (he can smell a fake one coming from a mile away), and you'll get his attention.

Ego stroking aside, what Leo really appreciates is a good joke and a bold spirit. He loves to laugh, and when looking for a new friend to add to his collection, he wants a partner in crime who lives their life boldly. Prove yourself loyal, too, and Leo will have a hard time letting you go.

D-I-S-R-E-S-P-E-C-T: Leo Friendship Dislikes

Being the friendly and faithful creature that he is, it takes a lot for Leo to unfriend someone. However, Leo cannot stand for someone taking a shot at his pride. Feeling good about himself means the world to the lion, so if a friend is constantly taking jabs at him, causing him to feel bad about his choices, he will simply banish them.

Disloyalty doesn't fly with Leo, either. Gossiping behind his back, spilling his secrets, or sabotaging his good name is more than enough for you to get booted from the pride. If you can't be loyal to him, then he won't feel loyal to you.

Coming in Hot: How Leo Handles Conflict

Leo's rage is a slow simmer. He might not pounce right away, but in the midst of a conflict, you better believe the intensity is building. Usually it's your Leo friend who will it take upon himself to take a breath in order to collect his thoughts, because he knows a searing growl is coming.

Leo isn't afraid of confrontation, and will say exactly what's on his mind—be it good, bad, or even ugly. His bluntness isn't out of malice, but out of the understanding that honesty is the only way to get to the bottom of the conflict. However, Leo has trouble with backing down, so he'll wait for you to raise the white flag before retreating to his den. Keep in mind that the more you try to defend yourself against Leo's bite, the more aggressive he'll become.

If you want to keep the peace, it's best to act with compassion and understanding. Offer him an apology (if it feels right), but above all else, allow him space to process his feelings before talking again. Despite his fierceness, Leo is actually a giant kitten, and his anger is often triggered by an emotional wound. Deep down, he wants to forgive and forget. While it might take a few days for him to come around again, he will, and you can rest assured that while Leo can be ruthless, he doesn't hold grudges.

Confidence and Compliments: Maintaining Your Friendship with Leo

While Leo comes across as ultraconfident on the outside, on the inside, he can suffer from Imposter Syndrome. This means that sometimes he finds it hard to believe in himself, questioning whether he deserves what he has, and whether he truly has what it takes to do all the wonderful things he dreams of. This is why it's important to support your Leo friend and remind him of his greatness. Yes, Leo's ego is bigger than most, and dishing out compliments might seem like the last thing he needs, but understand that underneath his bravado is a sensitive sign who desires validation. Your encouragement and support will mean a lot to him, and will further cement his loyalty to you.

Additionally, your Leo friend adores being the center of attention, and, honestly, there's nothing you can do but accept that. Rather than feel annoyed when he requires the spotlight, appreciate your friend's larger-than-life energy and revel in his fascinating stories. And if you feel overshadowed by Leo, don't hold back: join him in the spotlight and take part in his antics. Chances are he will gladly accept you onto the floor.

For all his fun-loving ways, however, Leo can take himself very seriously. He is his own worst critic, and when caught up in a project, he can shut off the world around him until it's completed. While you should remember not to take his behavior personally when he's in this mood, you should also keep in mind that your Leo needs another "Leo" in his life sometimes— meaning a friend who takes on his trademark high-spirited energy when he becomes a little too serious. Invite him out to do something fun, or send him a funny text to jolt him out of his headspace. He will appreciate the effort.

At times, your Leo friend can also be fixated on being right (he is a fixed sign, after all). This explains why, whether he's dispensing advice or leading a project, he has a tendency to come across as patronizing, and will refuse to take no for an answer. If you're more flexible than your lion friend, working around his needs will help avoid any issues. However, if you find yourself in a situation where your friend's aggressive nature is making you feel uncomfortable, talk about it. Leo appreciates directness: he wants to know where he stands with you at all times.

> **BFF Bonus Points**
>
> When it comes to getting your Leo friend a gift, think *VIP*: the hottest locations (dinner at a posh restaurant to satisfy his epicurean side) and the liveliest events (a private party full of glitz and glamour). You can also play to his artsy side by treating him to the latest hit musical, or even a karaoke machine.

Friendship Compatibility

What signs make the best pals for one of the friendliest members of the zodiac? How can outgoing Leo create a solid relationship with the introverted Taurus? In this section, you will discover more details about Leo's compatibility matches and how he might make a friendship work with each Sun sign.

Leo and Aries

Let playtime begin! When these two fire signs come together, lots of laughs and adventures are to be had. Leo and Aries can easily keep up with each other, and their mutual dynamism means there's never a dull moment. In fact, they both get a kick out of competing with each other—as long as they can play nicely. Since both the lion and the ram have big egos, power struggles can arise, as neither wants to back down. Thankfully, their mutual appreciation of each other is strong enough to resolve any conflict they might have (which is a good thing, because both of their tempers are quite hot to handle).

Leo and Taurus

While Leo is outgoing and playful, and Taurus tends to be more of an introverted homebody, these two have more in common than some may assume. Both the lion and the bull love luxury, and can easily spend hours together visiting art galleries, dining at the best restaurants, and getting their hair done. Blessed with friendly dispositions, their mutual sunniness can weather any storm, like when Taurus has to deal with Leo's bossiness and Leo gets irritated with Taurus's sensible nature.

Leo and Gemini

It's like a comedy sketch when these two come together: tons of laughs at a mile per minute. The lion and the twin bring out the kid in each other, and will find the fun in just about anything they do. Leo also admires

Gemini's sharp mind, while Gemini appreciates Leo's style and creativity. They can easily stay up for hours talking and joking around. While Leo may occasionally dislike sharing Gemini's attention with the twin's many friends, and Gemini may find Leo's sizable ego frustrating, these two are able to laugh off any disagreement.

Leo and Cancer

These signs will take a while to warm up to each other. Leo can't quite figure out Cancer's sensitive nature, while Cancer is taken aback by Leo's brashness. Try as the lion might, it'll be hard for him to understand the crab's moodiness, and the crab will find the lion's constant positivity to be grating at times. However, Cancer can learn to lighten up from Leo, and Leo can learn to appreciate the smaller, quieter moments in life from Cancer. If they learn to appreciate each other's differences, their friendship will go the distance.

Leo and Leo

When two sunny lions come together, they can expect a lot of purring—as well as the occasional growl. These two know exactly how to scratch each other's bellies, and will delight in a friendship built on fun, laughter, and affection. However, the friendship thrives only as long as there is mutual respect, and with two big cats comes two big egos, so there are bound to be a few clashes. Staying honest with each other, as well as learning how to compromise, will help these lions stay together.

Leo and Virgo

This is a funny combination that may have people stopping in wonder. On the outside, these two signs couldn't be more different: Virgo is demure and serious, while Leo is loud and always laughing. Though there are differences aplenty, they'll bond over their preference for perfection and diligent follow-through. In fact, the more time they spend time together, the better. Virgo will bring grounding to Leo's flights of fancy, and Leo can help Virgo crack a smile once in a while.

Leo and Libra

Leo and Libra are the social butterflies of the zodiac. They love people almost as much as they love themselves—and each other. Libra loves Leo's joie de vivre and social connections, while Leo admires Libra's sophistication and sense of humor. Both appreciate the arts and culture, and enjoy attending concerts, movies, and theater productions together. However, not all will be perfect in paradise. Leo may tire of Libra's incessant indecision, while Libra will be taken aback by Leo's brashness. Keeping things light and airy will ensure this friendship is on the right track.

Leo and Scorpio

Two of the most passionate signs in the zodiac equals one *intense* friendship. Both Leo and Scorpio demand a lot of attention and affection, which might be difficult to find in each other. Leo also finds Scorpio's intense privacy to be confusing, while Scorpio dislikes Leo's dramatic flair. Arguments may become full-out battles if both sides opt to remain stubborn. If Leo remembers his fascination with Scorpio's mind, and Scorpio appreciates Leo's warmth, it may save the connection.

Leo and Sagittarius

This is a classic BFF combination. These playful and adventurous souls delight in each other's company and are destined to take many trips together. Leo is inspired by Sagittarius's independent spirit, while Sagittarius admires Leo's regal vibe. Though they have their differences, they know that it's their diversity that makes them stronger. Leo offers security and protection to Sagittarius, while Sagittarius can broaden Leo's horizons.

Leo and Capricorn

Because they both demand authority, these two might have trouble connecting at first. Leo doesn't play second fiddle, and neither does Capricorn. However, if they can realize they are stronger together than they are apart, Leo and Capricorn can take on the world as a team. The lion will also benefit from the sea goat's cautious nature, while the sea goat's imagination can go to new heights thanks to the lion's creativity. Once they stop competing, they have plenty to talk about, and can make each other laugh with a ton of inside jokes. Plus, their sense of loyalty is unmatched.

Leo and Aquarius

Leo and Aquarius are astrological opposites, and it's not hard to see why. Leo is the star of his own show, focused on ensuring his future is secure and lavish. Aquarius is a supporting player who wants to save the world for the future of humankind. The lion doesn't gel with the water bearer's aloof nature, while the water bearer can't stand the lion's overbearing nature. Because both signs are loyal and crave stability in their friendships, they can find common ground if they respect each other's differences.

When Stars Align
If Aquarius wants a friendship to last with Leo, he shouldn't interfere with the lion's life choices, no matter how much he may disagree with them. He should voice his concerns, but then let it lie.

Leo and Pisces

Leo sees Pisces as his cub: he wants to protect her sensitive nature as best he can with his mighty roar. Pisces, meanwhile, sees Leo as a loyal friend whom she wants to lend a sympathetic ear to whenever he has a rare moment of vulnerability. While the flightiness of Pisces might make Leo feel uneasy, and Pisces may cower from Leo's bite, these two creative signs can make beautiful music together—literally and figuratively. Their conjoined genius knows no bounds.

Friendship Planets: Venus and Jupiter

To get the full scope of a friend or particular friendship, look at where the planets Venus and Jupiter align in your friend's and your charts. Venus rules love in all of its forms, including friendship. It indicates *how* you love others. Jupiter, meanwhile, indicates how you *show* your love. The planet of optimism, success, and generosity, it nudges you to experience new things and give to others.

Venus in Leo

The natural warmth and magnetic personality of Venus in Leo draws others in like moths to a flame, which explains why he has multiple circles of friends from different walks of life. He also goes out of his way to make connections with those he finds intriguing. He loves friends who are as bold as he is, and finds it difficult to be with those who settle for a life of monotony.

Extremely generous, Venus in Leo loves showering his friends with tokens of affection, whether it's surprising them with the perfect gift, or paying a warm compliment. He takes pride in making someone's day. However, while his affection is hard to refuse, he demands to be adored at the same level. If he feels he isn't, his insecurity can drive a wedge in his friendships. He also prefers pals who won't mind stepping aside so he can take the spotlight. After all, he is the star.

Jupiter in Leo

Spontaneous and creative, Jupiter in Leo is always up for something fun. He easily takes on the leadership role in his friendships, and knows exactly how to get things done. He has big ideas, so when he puts something on—like a birthday party or a networking event—it's going to be the biggest event of the year. Jupiter in Leo is also one for extravagant displays of affection, so he'll treat his friends to expensive gifts, and won't mind dropping a lot of money on a vacation with his best friend. Basically, his philosophy on life is "go big or go home," and he definitely doesn't want to stay at home—especially when he could be doing something fun with his friends. Jupiter in Leo runs the risk of appearing like a braggart, or someone who is hard to please, by those closest to him, however, which is why it's important for him to turn his confidence into a source of motivation. Encouraging his friends to dream bigger will make his value as a friend priceless.

Chapter 6

Virgo

(August 23–September 22)

Ruled by Mercury, the messenger of the gods and the planet of communication and intellect, Virgo is whip-smart. With an insatiable thirst for knowledge, her unmatched brainpower is always ten steps ahead of everyone else. Your Virgo pal doesn't mind digging deep into any and all of your issues—from your latest breakup to your career woes—and will offer analytical and observant advice.

The Perfectionist

Your Virgo friend is pretty picky. There's attention to detail—and then there's *Virgo's* attention to detail. However, don't mistake Virgo's precision for haughtiness. After all, she is an earth sign, which means she is grounded, practical, and relatable. Her perfectionism is also helped by her astrological symbol, the virgin. The virgin represents purification, control, and following the rules. This orderly energy is what prompts Virgo's love for organization and efficiency, whether it is to clean out her closet or complete a work task. However, amid her tidiness and productivity, Virgo understands that the most important work you can do in your lifetime is the work you do on yourself. When the going gets tough, Virgo wants to be prepared no matter what. That is why it's as common to find Virgo getting lost in a pile of books at a library as it is to spot her getting her sweat on at the gym: she's faithfully committed to her personal growth, and wants her physical body to be as sharp as her mind.

While her obsessive-compulsiveness might make things like dining out problematic at times (she won't hesitate to send something back again and again if it doesn't measure up to her expectations), her sharp eye is incredibly helpful when it comes to planning things like vacations, special events, and joint ventures. You'll appreciate her meticulousness when she scores you a deal on a luxe five-star hotel room, organizes your clothing, or notices a grammatical error in your cover letter. After all, your Virgo friend seeks perfection not only in herself but in everyone around her. She won't hesitate to tell you when you're not living up to your potential. Keep in mind that she will point this out not because she is being mean or nitpicky, but because she believes in your ability to reach your highest potential as deeply as she believes in her own. Underneath Virgo's cool and calm exterior lies a warm, soft heart yearning to help others.

The Doer

To say that Virgo is a hard worker would be an understatement. Virgo doesn't dream; she gets things done. And once she is committed to a particular task, there is no prying her away from it until it's completed to her impeccably high standards. While Mercury's influence gives Gemini a natural talent for a number of different pursuits (you may call him a jack-of-all-trades), the planet gives Virgo a steadfast, almost stubborn energy that allows her to excel in (and obsess over) one specific area or topic of interest. This means she won't stray from something until she's the best at it (just like Beyoncé, who is also a Virgo). Give your Virgo friend a job to complete—being your maid of honor/best man, creating your small business website, doing your taxes (she's great at numbers)—and she will do so with swift mental acuity and an energy so focused you'll be left in awe. However, Virgo isn't boastful; rather, she stays humble and quiet about her achievements. You might not even know what she was working on until someone else lets slip that it was her doing.

Virgo is also a mutable sign, which means she was born at the transition of one season (summer) into another (fall). As a mutable sign, your Virgo friend is highly adaptable and resourceful, and instinctively knows how to make things better in almost every situation. Don't be fooled by her sanitary appearance: she's not afraid to roll up her sleeves and get her hands a little dirty. As a natural problem-solver, Virgo is always ready to help you, whether you need to put together a couch, or bake three dozen cupcakes for a charity bake sale.

Written in the Stars

Virgo loves to keep her mind active so she can test out and improve her mental prowess. No wonder she's a big fan of games. Challenge her to checkers, an exciting whodunit, or even a video game, and you'll have her attention for hours.

Virgo Quirks: The Honorable Virgin

Virgo is symbolized by the virgin, which represents modesty, humanity, and a deep sense of duty and honor. You might even tease that your Virgo friend is like Mother Teresa (a fellow Virgo, by the way). In order to better understand your friend, however, you must know that Virgo needs to be of use in order to feel good about herself. She believes she is here for a specific purpose, and wants to help the world around her, including her loved ones, in the best way she can. No wonder your Virgo friend is always quick to lend a hand or offer you advice. She will go above and beyond to help out a friend, whether it's packing their belongings for a cross-country move, or staying up late to sort out a tricky personal problem—and she never expects anything in return.

However, for all of her good intentions, your Virgo friend's stalwart support runs the risk of coming across as self-righteous. You might roll your eyes as she offers her precise observations and sound advice time and again, and wonder if your friend is ever wrong about *anything*. The interesting thing is, the struggle is equally as real for Virgo herself. She is as hard on herself as she is on the people around her (if not more so), due to her belief that she has the potential for greatness. Virgo feels every minute not spent working toward improvement of some kind is a waste, which is extremely upsetting for her. This intense sense of duty is a heavy cross for Virgo to bear, and that weight can add a ton of pressure to her life. This may explain why she is prone to anxiety attacks and blue moods. However, it's this acute self-awareness that will lead her to her life's purpose, and a purposeful Virgo is a peaceful Virgo.

Narrow-Minded and Neat

"Just the facts, ma'am" is a typical Virgo quote. Her lust for knowledge might make her a great scholar, but she's also inherently skeptical. If you'd like your Virgo friend to say, "I believe you," without knowing all the facts, you'll be sorely disappointed. She lives her life by the book, and abides by the "I have to see it to believe it" adage. Undoubtedly, this can lead to arguments about who's "right" and who's "wrong," and Virgo hates being wrong, because she seldom is. After all, she always does her homework on the subject. Virgo puts in all of this work because she's initially suspicious of almost everything and everyone around her. No wonder it's hard getting to know her at first! She won't welcome a new friendship or new perspective until she's done her own thorough investigation into whether or not it is legitimate, and, of course, lives up to her code of standards.

And, yes, those standards are sky-high, especially when it comes to cleanliness. Yep, your Virgo friend is a real neat freak, as you may have already noticed. She hates dirt with such a passion that she often has trouble concentrating when she is in a messy or cluttered area. So don't be surprised if she vetoes a hotel room or restaurant because it is too "icky." Virgo's keen eye for detail means everything has its proper place and order; it doesn't matter whether you understand her methodology, as long as it makes sense to her—and she is all about things making sense.

Not surprisingly, Virgo is excellent at sticking to routines, because habits equals order. Her desire for order also includes the internal mechanisms of any given thing. She must understand why and how things work, including herself. Interestingly enough, for all of her skepticism, your Virgo friend enjoys dipping into books on philosophy and spirituality, as she seeks the answers to why she is who she is. Though it might seem like she has it all together on the outside, she is often dealing with intense internal purging, as she determines what needs to be removed in order for her life to run even more smoothly.

While Virgo's altruistic tendencies might annoy you at times, her dedication to living her truth, inside and out, may inspire you to conduct your own "life inventory," which is never a bad thing. Suffice to say you and your Virgo friend can easily stay up late into the night having deep conversations and philosophizing about your life's purpose—as she reorganizes your kitchen cupboards.

The Quiet Go-Getter: Where You'll Meet Virgo

Virgo finds comfort in knowledge, facts and figures, and the small details of life—anything that stimulates her mind and helps her achieve something. From a library to a knitting group, you'll spot her wherever there is something to learn. She's the type of person who enjoys discovering new things for the fun of it.

Because she loves all things holistic as well (a part of her quest to self-understanding), she might also be in your Pilates class, vegetarian cooking class, or meditation circle.

Virgo is also very kind and compassionate, and loves to help those in need, especially animals. Don't be surprised if you find her at an animal shelter or city farm. She is also a highly creative sign, and will be drawn to artistic activities like writing, poetry, and music. Keep an eye out for her in your writing workshop or painting class!

No matter what she's doing, Virgo is quietly intense about the task at hand. She keeps her head down and will diligently work away, almost in a trance. She doesn't like drawing much attention to herself, and, thanks to her tunnel vision, she also doesn't pay a whole lot of attention to those around her, either. Shy and reserved, she won't be found in big group activities.

Written in the Stars

While Virgo enjoys traveling, she still needs to feel productive—even when on vacation. She prefers to keep active and mentally stimulated, which means she'll plan a packed itinerary with plenty to see and do. Tokyo and Lisbon are ideal cities for Virgo to visit.

Nice and Slow: How to Become Friends with Virgo

Don't overpower Virgo. As a humble and down-to-earth sign, she will be put off by anything she deems aggressive or showy. Instead, try giving her a quick smile and nod of acknowledgment during your first few meetings before finally approaching her. Also keep in mind that it's difficult for her to make small talk. She actually hates it, and would much rather talk about things of significance—so skip the chitchat and ask a legitimate question about her job or pets (she loves talking about her pets). She also prefers one-on-one encounters, so keep your meet-ups just between the two of you at first.

Don't be offended if Virgo rejects the first two or three invitations to lunch. While she is friendly, she's also very protective of herself, which means she is very picky of whom she lets into her tight circle of friends. She takes both privacy and longevity seriously, so she has something of a vetting process to ensure her tribe members can be trusted through and through. Prove yourself to be a loyal and discreet person to Virgo, and you'll have yourself a forever friend.

Nosey and Noisy: Virgo Friendship Dislikes

It takes time for Virgo to open up, which is why it's important for her to be able to trust her friends with private information, including the inner workings of her heart and soul. Nothing infuriates Virgo more than when she suspects someone of digging into her personal affairs out of pure salaciousness, or when she learns someone is gossiping about her behind her back. If proven guilty of such offences, you'll instantly be cut out from her group.

Being loud and obnoxiously gregarious is another turnoff for Virgo. She prefers quiet and calm conversations, and understated activities. If you consistently draw attention to yourself and insist on chatting nonstop (especially about nonsense), Virgo will shut off the noise by leaving for good.

Demure Debater: How Virgo Handles Conflict

Virgo typically shies away from confrontation. She is a peacekeeper, and would rather quickly reach a resolution than deal with a full-out war. However, an attack against her integrity is more than enough provocation for her. Don't underestimate her quiet nature: if you say something that she knows isn't true, or accuse her of wrongdoing without any substantial evidence, she won't hesitate to speak up.

Your Virgo friend never enters an argument unless she knows she can win, and thanks to her intellect and quick mind, she'll probably win a lot. With her back pocket filled with facts, and a passion for justice, arguing with Virgo will make you feel like you're in court, debating a lawyer. Even when fighting, however, Virgo seldom gets riled up; her demeanor usually remains nonchalant and composed. Although, she *will* fight to get the last word in, because that is a Virgo must. Thankfully, she hates tension, so she's quick to make up. Keep the following in mind though: hurt her, and she'll never forgive or forget.

Calm and Compassion: Maintaining Your Friendship with Virgo

Because your Virgo friend is so analytical and critical about, well, everything, she tends to live in her head a lot and has trouble moving away from her routines. It's a great idea to gently jolt her from her racing headspace and day-to-day schedule once in a while by encouraging her to try something different from her norm. Anything connected to her physical body, like dancing or hiking, is a good start. Virgo also tends to be reserved and cautious, even around those whom she trusts the most. Being vulnerable is difficult for her despite how deeply she feels. Providing a safe space for your Virgo friend to speak freely and share her feelings and fears is extremely valuable to her, and will help your friendship evolve.

Being that Virgo gives so selflessly and so deeply desires to be of service to her nearest and dearest, it's important to acknowledge and appreciate your Virgo friend's giant heart. While it's true she helps out because of her adoration for you and not for the accolades, it's important for her to know that she is, indeed, helping, and that what she does matters. Even sending a simple-yet-sincere thank-you note or text will mean the world to your Virgo pal.

Virgo is also a natural worrywart. She worries about almost everything, from the bus running late to her pants not matching her shirt. Mostly, however, she worries about being a failure to herself and to her loved ones. It's her inner perfectionist that causes her to look at herself with this extremely critical eye. This is why the biggest gift you can give to your Virgo friend is the reminder that she is doing the best she can with the knowledge she has. There is nothing more she can do, because she truly is great as is. Essentially, playing the role of cheerleader to counter her inner critic will help your friendship grow in positive ways.

BFF Bonus Points

As a picky perfectionist, Virgo is hard to shop for, but focusing on her astrological tendencies can help you score the right gift. Since she rarely relaxes, a spa day is just what the doctor ordered. You can also cater to her inner health freak by gifting her personal training sessions or cooking classes.

Friendship Compatibility

Can practical Virgo connect with the romantic Libra? What makes Virgo's bond with Scorpio so special? The following section sheds light on each of Virgo's best compatibility matches, as well as how she operates in a friendship with those Sun signs that are not part of her top friend matches.

Virgo and Aries

Both Virgo and Aries like to be of service to others, and can bond over volunteer work or a joint cause. However, the similarities seem to end there. Virgo is very conscious of what she says and how she behaves, which is essentially the opposite of Aries. While the virgin might appreciate the ram's support in pushing her to new heights, and the ram values the virgin's problem-solving skills, an element of true connection appears to be missing, which may make it difficult for their friendship to evolve.

Virgo and Taurus

These earth signs have a lot more in common than what first meets the eye. While Virgo might think Taurus is too lethargic at times, and Taurus doesn't like Virgo's intensely critical eye, they share a special bond, both enjoying the finer things in life, as well as quality time spent exploring the great outdoors. Because they both also value stability, this bond is built on a firm foundation that can last forever.

Virgo and Gemini

While Virgo and Gemini are both ruled by Mercury, they could not be more different. The twin has a high-strung energy that easily drives the virgin bananas, while the virgin's quest for perfection irritates the heck out of the twin. However, they admire each other's intelligence, and they may find themselves lost in deep conversations together for hours on end. This connection is perfect for when each sign craves mental stimulation.

Virgo and Cancer

Both Virgo and Cancer might appear emotionless at times, but they feel so much more than what they reveal to others. It's this emotional understanding that helps cement their connection. As homebodies who prefer quiet nights in, the virgin and the crab will find they have plenty to bond over. Virgo appreciates Cancer's thoughtfulness, while Cancer admires Virgo's principles. Communicating this respect for each other will help this friendship thrive.

Virgo and Leo

Virgo and Leo are a unique pair. Virgo is bashful, while is Leo is bodacious. The virgin prefers to remain in the background, while the lion must take center stage. Yet it's precisely these differences that can make this friendship work. These two know where they stand with each other, so competition is rare. However, Virgo may tire of stroking Leo's ego, and Leo may grow irritated with Virgo's uptight nature. However, their .mutual love for animals—particularly cats—may help purr-fect this friendship.

Virgo and Virgo

A friendship between two Virgos can either be the friendship of a lifetime—or a lifetime sentence. Both are intelligent and curious creatures, and the conversations they share will not only touch on a variety of subjects, but also last into the wee hours of the night. Being in nature also lifts their spirits, and they make excellent traveling companions. However, two Virgos makes for double the criticism, which could drive a wedge between them. It's best for them to offer only constructive criticism, or say nothing at all.

When Stars Align

Virgos are bound to criticize each other behind their backs if they're not able to communicate their needs face-to-face. Remember, honesty is the best policy.

Virgo and Libra

Virgo and Libra confuse each other. Virgo doesn't understand how Libra can see the world through rose-colored glasses, and Libra doesn't understand what Virgo is fussing about all of the time. Given the opportunity to speak freely, Virgo would label Libra flaky, and Libra would call Virgo a wet blanket. While they admire each other's intelligence and can offer insightful advice into the other's woes, this friendship will require a lot of communication skills to excel.

Virgo and Scorpio

A wonderfully weird combination, Virgo appreciates how deeply Scorpio can connect to her feelings, while Scorpio appreciates the precision by which Virgo lives her life. Together, they can help improve each other's worlds for the better. Virgo also values Scorpio's support and uncanny ability to understand her, and Scorpio loves how Virgo can help her reorganize her life from the outside in. It's the kind of friendship TV series are made from.

Virgo and Sagittarius

Virgo and Sagittarius have the best of intentions when it comes to their friendship, but there's a few obstacles standing in their way. For starters, Virgo doesn't relate to Sagittarius's grandiose demeanor, while Sagittarius is easily put out by Virgo's reserve. Virgo also likes to play it safe, while Sagittarius is all about taking risks. And discussions on hot topics never go well, as both signs believe that their point of view is the "correct" one. However, both the virgin and the archer are incredibly sharp and share a passion for philosophical books and movies. When they appreciate each other's differences, they make amazing travel partners that can go the distance.

When Stars Align

During a discussion, Sagittarius should remember to take a breath and let Virgo have the floor once in a while; otherwise, Virgo will soon tire of Sagittarius's self-indulgent diatribe.

Virgo and Capricorn

While there might be some differences between them—Virgo dislikes Capricorn's bossiness, and Capricorn tires of Virgo's brooding—these two earth signs know they can count on each other no matter what. They appreciate each other's loyalty and stability, and always enjoy themselves no matter what they're doing, from going hiking to attending concerts together. Even if distance (or a job change) comes between them, they know they'll always have each other's back.

Virgo and Aquarius

For all of their differences—Virgo craves order and routine, while Aquarius thrives on chaos—the virgin and the water bearer find common ground when it comes to being of service to others. They also bond over their passion for bettering themselves, and will enjoy working out together and swapping healthy recipes. However, Aquarius's ideas can be too "out there" for Virgo, and Virgo's narrow-mindedness may annoy Aquarius. For this friendship to really grow, it is best for these signs to focus on specific tasks to work on together, such as training for a charity race.

Virgo and Pisces

Astrological opposites, Virgo and Pisces initially have trouble connecting. Virgo's skepticism frustrates dreamy Pisces, while Pisces's scatterbrained nature irritates ultraorganized Virgo. However, once they're able to recognize that their strengths can help each other—Pisces's big heart will uplift Virgo, while Virgo's creativity will inspire Pisces—these two can form a friendship that will surprise even themselves. Both compassionate signs, they will bond over serving others, like volunteering at an animal shelter.

Friendship Planets: Venus and Jupiter

Considering the planets of Venus and Jupiter in your friend's and your charts, in addition to the Sun signs, can help you gain a better understanding of your friendship and how you both operate as friends. Venus rules love and unions of all kinds, including friendships. It reflects *how* you love others. Jupiter indicates how you *show* your love to your friends. The planet of optimism, success, and generosity, Jupiter's influence nudges you to open yourself up to new experiences and friendships.

Venus in Virgo

Venus in Virgo initially comes across as cautious and reserved to others. This difficulty with opening up to others stems from her fear of being hurt—and she will avoid being hurt at all costs. This may explain why she has such high standards when it comes to selecting those who'll make the cut for her squad. Once she feels safe and secure, however, she is an extremely loyal friend. While she wears a poker face quite well, inwardly she is very sensitive. This doesn't stop her from being critical of others, though, and she won't hesitate to point out what's not working in her friends' lives. She does this not because she's uncaring, but because she cares so much, and is always trying to help her friends better themselves.

Venus in Virgo also wants to feel needed and useful in her friendships, and it makes her feel good to treat her friends to small, thoughtful gifts and gestures. She doesn't require much in return from her friends, mainly just their loyalty and respect, as well as their ability to be discreet. Drama queens (or kings) need not apply.

Jupiter in Virgo

Jupiter in Virgo is helpful, honest, and practical. She succeeds when she is organizing things and adhering to the meticulous details, which is why she's the point person for putting together special events like birthday parties and vacations. She motivates those around her by doing—she doesn't just talk the talk; she walks the walk. While she's not much of a risk-taker, she is always true to her word, and her discipline helps inspire others around her.

Jupiter in Virgo also enjoys being of service to others, so her friends know they can count on her to help them out, whether it's moving furniture or accompanying them to a doctor's appointment. Her ability to grasp facts and problem-solve explains why she is so good at dispensing the soundest advice to her friends whenever they're in a jam. However, her need to always be by the book can come across as sterile and unfeeling. One of the biggest life lessons for Jupiter in Virgo is to let her guard down and allow herself to be vulnerable, especially with her nearest and dearest.

Chapter 7

Libra
(September 23–October 22)

The person voted "Most Popular" in your high school was most likely a Libra. It's easy to fall under the naturally charming Libra's spell. Ruled by Venus, the planet of love, Libra thrives in a harmonious and affectionate environment, one which is preferably also visually stunning, because your Libra friend adores beautiful things. Once you make it on his VIP list, you have a friend for life.

The Social Butterfly

As his ruling planet Venus dictates, Libra is all about love. He loves being around people, and spreading good cheer. And as the most graceful air sign, he is also #blessed with the gift of the gab, impeccable manners, and social charms—it's no wonder he shines the brightest when he's around others. His diplomatic zodiac symbol, the scales, also permits Libra to believe that two heads are always better than one, and he lives with the understanding that nothing is more valuable in life than cooperation and unity. Couple that with the fact that he is a cardinal sign (meaning his sign begins a new season—fall—and represents initiation and action), and your Libra friend's mission in life is bringing different groups of people together. This can be for a special event or cause, or even just a regular Friday night, so don't be surprised if a quiet game night with your Libra friend turns into a big blowout with multiple invitees.

Fun-loving and eternally youthful, he initiates conversations easily, asking questions with a childlike curiosity, and sees dialogue as a means to build relationships. In fact, it is thanks to his effortless, thoughtful communication skills that he has so many friends from different age groups and walks of life. He abides by the adage "the more the merrier," and is his most joyous self when surrounded by people, talking and laughing for hours. As long as there is love and a lot of fun to be had, Libra will welcome you with open arms.

Libra's warm nature is also useful to those who are more introverted and shy. If social situations make you uncomfortable, your affable Libra friend has no trouble taking you by the arm and graciously introducing you to everyone in the room, ensuring that everyone knows who you are. Libra lives to make a good impression— and wants to help you make one as well.

Written in the Stars

Libra adores cultural events. From an art gallery to the ballet to the symphony, he loves art in all of its forms, particularly if it's refined and elegant. And if he can score box seats, even better. Too chichi for you? The latest historical-romance flick will also do.

The Peacekeeper

Whenever there's a conflict within your friend group, Libra undoubtedly steps up as the mediator. Libra's element is air, which means he's blessed with effective communication skills, superior intelligence, and the ability to make decisions using his head rather than his heart. Because it's so easy for him to detach himself from any given issue, he is able to analyze the situation with objectivity and fairness. And, as his symbol indicates, Libra is all about being fair. If someone is being treated unjustly, your Libra pal will do whatever he can to make it right. Even if a friend refuses to compromise, Libra will compromise for them. He's driven by balance, so if something is even teetering the scales a little bit, he will make up the difference.

While Libra is one of the best diplomats of the zodiac—and everyone needs a good diplomat on their side—his cooperative nature can go a little too far at times. At his worst, Libra is a people-pleaser, desperate to accommodate everyone in order to keep the peace. As he compromises and is often quick to agree with others, you might wonder at times what exactly your Libra friend stands for.

Libra Quirks: The Shallow Scales

"Mirror, mirror on the wall, who is the fairest one of all?" Your Libra friend will answer, "Me, of course." But with such impeccable taste, who could blame him? Libra enjoys the finer things in life, from his sophisticated wardrobe to his deluxe waffle maker. You can be sure that his gadgets are top of the line, because Libra only wants the best for the best (and Libra believes he is the best). While you might admire his self-confidence, your Libra friend's vanity can be irritating at times for friends who simply want a quiet casual night out and don't understand his incessant need to preen, charm, and impress everyone wherever he goes.

The truth is, Libra has a shiny veneer that often hides a darker reality: he's scared of not being loved by others. However, he doesn't want you to know this about him. Unlike Leo, the loud and proud lion, the scales tends to pretend that everything is fine in order to make the best impression possible. He may also throw himself into certain acts to ensure that when something isn't going well in his life, his status in the minds of others remains elevated. This can include collecting intel on people and seizing opportunities that he believes will make you, and everyone else, like him more. For example, he might hate peanut butter and jelly sandwiches with a passion, but will say he likes them because you do. Or he might wrangle tickets to a concert he would otherwise not go to because he knows you really wanted to attend. Is he buying your friendship? Kind of, but he doesn't really mean to. It's important to know that your Libra friend's actions don't come from a place of malicious, but rather a deep need for validation and connection.

Cheerleader and Curator

At the heart of Libra is, well, his big heart. He is the inspiring champion of love, the head coach who will endlessly cheer on his team. Libra makes an incredible leader because he's so devoted to harmony and #good-vibes. Your Libra friend instinctively knows how to rally the troops in times of crisis, and is the first to spread loving-kindness. When you are having a down day, he is the first to give you that much-needed pep talk.

A relentless optimist, it's no wonder that Libra, the air sign that he is, is constantly living with his head in the clouds, daydreaming of storybook scenarios. And as the romantic of the zodiac, he will go above and beyond to live out those fantasies. For example, your Libra pal might imagine hosting a picturesque Friendsgiving that, while most will find extreme, he will insist upon doing because it looks so dreamy and *Instagram*-worthy. While his dreaminess might cause some annoyance for his friends, especially for those who prefer that things be more laid back (how many times must you pose for the same picture, after all?), those closest to him know that he does make life more beautiful.

It is no wonder, then, that Libra consciously curates everything in his life, from his fashion to his furniture. Quality and aesthetics are important to Libra: he needs everything to look "just so." His love of beautiful things extends to the beauty that is man-made, like works of art, as well as the natural beauty that surrounds him, like a perfect sunrise. This love of pleasure and indulgence might come across as overzealous at times, but it can also be inspiring. Take cues from his enviable closet and epicurean nose, and you are sure to improve your own tastes.

Thanks to his high intelligence and easy conversation skills, he seamlessly segues between different social groups and situations, which is why you'll want to take your Libra friend as your wing-person for a film premiere, an art auction, or a high-profile charity event. He'll dazzle everyone with his knowledge and contagious smile. Well, maybe not *everyone*... Some friends might feel that Libra's constant need for aesthetic perfection can outshine their own attempts at beauty and style. However, it's important to remember that Libra doesn't mean to incite any competition; he is just doing what comes perfectly naturally to him: looking good.

Most Popular: Where You'll Meet Libra

From a lively debate club to a crowded newsroom to a busy restaurant, chances are you'll meet your Libra friend where there are tons of people and lots to talk about. Libra brings his gift of the gab and his charming self to every activity he does. He also loves the VIP treatment, so you may also find him at ribbon-cutting ceremonies or top-secret special events. An exuberant patron of the fine arts, it's also likely you'll meet Libra while strolling through an art gallery or a fashion exhibit. He loves to be around people and things that inspire him and ignite his vivid imagination.

Without even knowing his sign, you'll be instantly attracted to Libra. While he isn't the loudest or most demonstrative in a group setting (that would be the assertive Aries or the dramatic Leo), he is certainly the most popular. Libra gets along with everyone, from the mail room attendant to the CEO. You'll recognize him by his easygoing nature, superb listening skills, and uncanny magnetism.

Flattery and Openness: How to Become Friends with Libra

While Libra will undoubtedly initiate a conversation with you—since he must meet everyone in a room—it would behoove you to open with a compliment. Flattery will get you everywhere when it comes to approaching or receiving Libra. He lives to be admired. Of course, it won't be very hard to do so; no doubt, you'll already appreciate his choice of clothing, or how he handled himself in a tricky display of verbiage. Don't be afraid to ask him questions either, including (polite) personal ones; Libra secretly loves talking about himself. Because he's a chatty air sign, engaging him in a light-hearted debate will also earn his affection.

In general, you can be unguarded with Libra. Because he is open to interacting with different people from different walks of life, he respects people who show up to the event with an open heart and an open mind, as well as those who make him feel special (considering the time he puts into his fashion sense, he doesn't mind his ego being stroked a bit). Ultimately, like the Venusian he is, Libra enjoys establishing genuine connections with people. He is all about making relationships, so he will do his best to be a good friend to those who show the same effort.

Sloppy Sloths: Libra Friendship Dislikes

Libra likes friends who are kind and social, with a penchant for good grooming. He doesn't care for sloppiness. Libra is the typical Venusian, and thus loves beautiful things and people; physical appearance and making good impressions are important to him. Embarrass him with your careless choice of clothing or uncouth behavior, and you'll surely be demoted. A sensitive soul, Libra also dislikes being criticized, especially about his own physical characteristics. What you may deem a small offhand remark about his appearance will cut deep, and is enough for you to be taken off his Christmas list. And while Libra doesn't expect his friends to be as popular as he is, he certainly prefers that they enjoy the same level of social interaction as he does. Homebodies who constantly rebuff his invitations need not apply.

Ghosting and Grudges: How Libra Handles Conflict

As the peacemaker of the zodiac, Libra doesn't do well with conflict of any sort. If something is bothering you,

Libra will do just about anything in order to come to an agreement or compromise before the situation escalates into a full-fledged fight. His need for balance and keeping things as harmonious as possible means he would rather take flight than fight. This also explains why if it's Libra who has the issue, he prefers to sweep things under the carpet than deal with them head-on. As a result, it's difficult to air grievances and resolve your issues with Libra. However, as much as he avoids conflict like the plague, he can still feel a great deal of anger and annoyance. Libra also won't hesitate to hold a grudge if he feels he has been personally violated or insulted in any way, e.g., if you forgot his birthday or failed to invite him to an exclusive networking event. Once he's done, he's done. Receiving any sort of explanation for his going AWOL will be nearly impossible.

Your best bet in handling a conflict with Libra is to bring up whatever's troubling you in a calm, collected manner. Let him know that you're open to a discussion and want to find a compromise as quickly as possible so you can both move forward. You're sure to kiss and make up in no time.

Sharing and Security: Maintaining Your Friendship with Libra

Libra loves to share. From food to clothing, he never hesitates to share anything and everything with his tribe, and he expects the same in return. This means if you order a tasty-looking dish at a restaurant, or own a stunning coat that's caught your Libra friend's attention, be prepared to offer him a bite and let him take your duds for a whirl. Rest assured he will serve you a sliver of his own dessert—and fashionable clothing is always safe in his hands. And speaking of fashion, Libra is definitely the friend who takes the longest getting ready. Frustrating? Yes. Can you do anything about it? Not really. Your best bet is to give him an additional window of time to prep and preen so you don't get mad at him for running late—and he doesn't get mad at you for rushing him.

Underneath Libra's happy-go-lucky exterior is someone who's also extremely fickle. It's not totally surprising: he does like his balance. This means he needs to be on his own just as much as he needs to be around people. So when your Libra friend suddenly goes MIA, don't take it personally. Just give him his space—he'll be back around before you know it! Your understanding will also be greatly appreciated.

Reminding your Libra friend of his inner strength is another gift you can give him (and one he might not realize he needs). Libra's desire for peace and harmony stems from his indecisiveness and fear that he will make the "wrong" choice, particularly if his decision affects those around him. He can be so focused on pleasing others, in fact, that he often neglects his own needs. Gently nudging your Libra friend to get out of his own way by encouraging him to trust his instincts and be a little less hard on himself is a kind gesture that will go a long way.

Friendship Compatibility

Can Libra find common ground with Capricorn? How might a friendship between two Libras flourish? The following section uncovers each of Libra's astrological friend matches, as well as how he might cultivate a relationship with a sign that is outside of these matches.

Libra and Aries

Astrological opposites, these two have more in common than meets the eye. Both alphas—they prefer to take the lead and have everyone's attention— these signs actually balance each other out quite well (no Libra pun intended). The scales likes the ram's passion and decisiveness, while the ram admires the scales' cooperative and kind nature. Though misunderstandings may be aplenty, thanks to that polarity energy, each sign brings to the friendship what the other is missing.

When working on a project with Libra, Aries needs to relinquish his control once in a while and try to make things as equal as possible.

Libra and Taurus

When Libra and Taurus come together, it's like peanut butter and jelly: they perfectly complement each other. Both ruled by Venus, these signs share a love of art, culture, and luxury. They love attending the hottest theater productions, concerts, and movies together, and will cohost one heck of an Oscar party. The scales is also able to smooth out the bull's stubbornness, while the bull helps the scales make decisions. Conflicts may arise, however, when stoic Taurus gets annoyed with chatterbox Libra, and Libra can't get homebody Taurus to go out on a Friday night. If these two can appreciate their differences, their friendship will blossom.

Libra and Gemini

These two air signs are made for each other. Their shared intellect, quick wit, and easy conversational skills means they can talk and laugh for hours on end. Both extroverts, the scales and the twin also enjoy making plans together that get them out of the house and around as many people as possible, like attending music festivals, nightclubs, and amusement parks. Thanks to their varied interests and boundless energy, there's never a dull moment with these two.

Libra and Cancer

Libra's often confused by Cancer's moodiness, and Cancer is intimidated by Libra's huge social circle—but that doesn't mean these two don't enjoy each other's company. In fact, their differences work best when collaborating on a project together, as Cancer appreciates Libra's charm and diplomacy when the going gets tough, and Libra values Cancer's self-awareness and creativity. While they might consider bonding in smaller doses, these two have the potential for a far-reaching friendship.

Libra and Leo

All hail Team Glam. When Libra and Leo sashay into a room, arm in arm, heads turn. These two love living the high life together, from food to fashion, and always look amazing. In fact, sharing beauty and fashion secrets with each other is one of their favorite things to do. However, Libra isn't a fan of Leo's bossiness, and Leo can't stand Libra's indecisiveness. If these two focus on bringing out the best in each other, rather than competing for the spotlight, their bond will be electric.

Libra and Virgo

Libra and Virgo are like two puzzle pieces that fit perfectly together—if they don't puzzle each other too much. Both signs appreciate beauty and culture, and enjoy going to art galleries and museums together. They also have a knack for fashion and will love borrowing each other's clothes. However, Libra may feel confined by Virgo's perfectionism and introversion, while Virgo will be daunted by Libra's intense social calendar and charming personality. If they can each adapt to the other's nature, this friendship will flourish.

Libra and Libra

Libras love themselves, and two Libras together definitely love each other. The scales is one sign that gets along with his own kind extremely well. These two find each other to be just as charming, funny, and smart as themselves, and love talking together for hours. One of the best aspects of this friendship is that neither likes to argue, so there's little chance of a heated argument between these two. However, Libra's trademark indecision may make it difficult for them to make concrete plans.

Libra and Scorpio

While different at their cores, these two signs can bring out the best in each other. Yes, Libra is lighthearted and carefree, while Scorpio is intense and emotional, but it's through these differences that each sign will shine. Libra finds Scorpio to be one of his most intriguing friends, while sharp-tongued Scorpio values Libra's natural diplomacy. Using Libra's head and Scorpio's heart, these two can tackle any obstacle together.

Libra and Sagittarius

While the archer's aggressive and ambitious nature is extreme for the refined and friendly scales, they ultimately appreciate each other for who they truly are. On top of which, Libra and Sagittarius both love to socialize and can try tons of new things together. They also make each other laugh, and easily support each other during tough times. Libra might not like Sagittarius's lack of tact, and Sagittarius will get annoyed with Libra's indecision, but these easygoing signs will always forgive and forget.

When Stars Align
The best way for Sagittarius to acquiesce Libra's indecisiveness? Simply make the decision on where to go on a Saturday night. Don't worry: easygoing Libra will always go along with the plan.

Libra and Capricorn

With little in common, Libra and Capricorn may have difficulty finding a middle ground. The practical sea goat is a little too serious for the friendly scales, and the scales' vanity will irk the grounded sea goat. Being cardinal signs, both enjoy taking charge, so there's bound to be a power struggle. However, these two can make each other laugh, and will love taking in Mother Nature together.

Libra and Aquarius

These two share a strong mental connection that is almost out of this world. They love taking yoga classes together, and enjoy stimulating conversations on a wide range of topics, from politics to pop culture. Both the scales and the water bearer also love helping people, and will like volunteering for a special cause together. Despite the heavy connection Libra and Aquarius share, they also know how to make each other laugh like no other, and excel when collaborating on a creative project together.

Libra and Pisces

These two creative souls may like daydreaming together, but there is little between them to ground their dreaminess. Libra feels stifled by Pisces's neediness, while Pisces is intimidated by Libra's ability to get along with everyone. Both signs are also indecisive, which can be frustrating when trying to make plans. However, Libra and Pisces are also both forgiving and loving, and if they establish good boundaries with each other, they can develop a great friendship.

Friendship Planets: Venus and Jupiter

Looking at where the planets of Venus and Jupiter are in your friend's and your charts, in addition to your

Sun signs, can further help you understand that friend and your friendship with them. Venus rules love and unions of all kinds, including friendships, and reflects *how* you love. Jupiter is the planet of optimism, success, and generosity, and indicates how you *show* your love to those you care about.

Venus in Libra

Venus in Libra is a people person, and he knows it. Thanks to his natural charm, wit, and conversational skills, he knows just how to make people feel comfortable. Everyone he meets is instantly attracted to his effervescent and warm energy. At a party, he is the one who's mingling and bringing people together, which he loves to do. Friends come to him for his advice, thanks to his diplomatic nature, and he loves offering his insight, especially concerning his friends' personal lives and styles. Venus in Libra's impeccable fashion sense is the envy of his friends, in fact, and he is only too happy to lend something from his closet to a friend in need, or help them refresh their wardrobe on a shopping spree.

Since he hates arguing and yearns to keep things balanced and harmonious in his friendships, Venus in Libra is usually the first person to compromise. He is drawn to people who are intelligent, well mannered, and well groomed just like him. Those who are arrogant and vulgar don't belong in his chic circle.

Jupiter in Libra

Jupiter in Libra is charming, positive, and fair-minded. His natural graciousness and diplomacy make him an excellent meditator, which is why he is the best person to settle any arguments within his social circle—and also why he prefers compromising and cooperating over fighting with his loved ones. His cleverness and ability to see both sides to every issue makes him especially adept at problem-solving. Because he is so good with people, he tends to have a large social circle. His need to be around other people means he likes connecting friends from different circles so they can be one big happy family—he might also have a bit of matchmaker within him.

Jupiter in Libra's artistic flair, as well as his penchant for fine foods, makes him the leading cultural expert in his squad; he loves introducing new restaurants and new music to his friends. While his confidence is revered by many, he might be something of an egoist, which can come across as patronizing and snobby at times. Keeping this tendency in check—while maintaining his jovial nature—will attract many friends to his life.

Chapter 8

Scorpio
(October 23–November 21)

Unapologetically intense and known for often getting lost in deep thought, signs don't get any deeper than Scorpio. She's the friend to call when you're facing an existential crisis or when you want to discuss all things deep, dark, and sexy. Thanks to her sharp intuition, she instinctively knows which friends are best suited for her. Beware: once you're in Scorpio's squad, you're there until death do you part.

The Enigma

Your Scorpio friend is an unsolved mystery. You can never quite figure her out. In one instant, she's independent and demands her space, and in the next, she's texting you constantly. She is passionate, and yet she's aloof; she's confident, and yet she's insecure. But she's not being difficult: she's complex, and just can't help it.

Scorpio is ruled by two planets: Mars and Pluto. As the planet of action and self-expression, Mars endows Scorpio with hunger, willpower, and self-reliance. Meanwhile, Pluto (also the ancient god of the underworld and judge of the dead) links Scorpio to all things connected to regeneration and transformation, including death, sex, and the occult. While most people shy away from what lies in these dark and often taboo places, Scorpio thrives here thanks to her ties to mysterious Pluto. Got a question for your Scorpio pal—she'll probably consult her tarot card deck first. But while she has respect for destiny, she also doesn't like being at the whim of forces that are beyond her control. Thanks to Mars, she has a strong desire to rule her own world, within her own timeline. Because of this, she is constantly testing herself; she sees life as something to be felt on every level, and while Mars gives her the will, Pluto teaches her about the mysteries of life and death.

Scorpio isn't afraid to feel and experience the dark, because she knows it will lead to the light. For example, she understands that failed relationships lead to healthier ones, and that losing a job only means there's a better one around the corner. In fact, Scorpio has a fantastic sense of humor when it comes to life's little (or big) mishaps, and her trademark sarcasm helps ease the pain—yours or her own.

Because of her dual planet placement, your Scorpio friend can also help you become more comfortable with the different facets of your own personality, as well as whatever life throws at you. She's the friend who will give you a precise perspective on life's tragedies and triumphs, and will offer you spiritual insights to help you see that there's more to life than meets the eye. She is also quick to offer you a parting hug because she understands that death can happen whenever, wherever. And if you need to talk about sex? You know who to call. Consider Scorpio your spiritual and sex guru.

The Investigator

Scorpio's intensity makes her pretty much a fanatic for whatever strikes her fancy. A probing creature, Scorpio makes a grade A researcher and scholar. As a fixed sign (meaning she was born at the height of a season—fall—and is determined, persistent, and stubborn), she also likes making lists and putting things in order. While an Aries pal might come up with the idea to take a vacation, it's your Scorpio friend who will research the vacation spot, accommodations, and activities, and put together a proposed itinerary. Like a dog chewing on a bone, once she's focused on a task, there's nothing that will stop Scorpio until she's uncovered whatever it is she's after.

Written in the Stars

Planning a trip with your Scorpio pal? While you'd be hard-pressed to get this natural homebody out of her room, Scorpio does enjoy visiting under-the-radar historical destinations that are both sexy and a little mysterious. She would love to travel to New Orleans, Montenegro, or Cuba.

Scorpio especially likes to tinker with what she doesn't understand, because exploring the unknown often leads her to a deeper understanding of herself. If you need help with any task that requires follow-through, research, or out-of-the-box thinking, message your Scorpio pal. She'll be happy to help you answer the big questions. With a nose for secrets—because she has so many of her own—your Scorpio friend also knows the good gossip, or where to find it. Need to vet a date? Curious about what your ex is up to? Scorpio will get the details.

Scorpio Quirks: The Straight-Up Scorpion

Your Scorpio friend doesn't mince words. Symbolized by the scorpion, she won't hesitate to strike with harsh truths when necessary. If she doesn't like your outfit, your partner, or your dog, she'll let you know. If you're in a pouty mood or behaving badly, Scorpio has no problem putting you in your place. While it's easy to label her as abrasive or unfeeling in these situations, you must know that your Scorpio friend says these things because she cares a lot about you. Really. The thing is, your scorpion pal knows that you deserve better. She knows you could dress better and date better, and would fare better with a cat. So she'll throw you some tough truth bombs, hoping you'll make a change and start anew.

While you might not always appreciate a scorpion's unsolicited criticism, if you're ready to transform your life, she will know exactly where to start and what to do. What Scorpio herself must learn is that she can't force people to change; she has to let her friends fight their own battles, even if she doesn't agree with their decisions.

Power, Privacy, and Overprotection

To Scorpio, power equals freedom, and freedom means she can be truly herself. Scorpio despises authority and domineering personalities. Being under someone's thumb means being stifled, which doesn't sit well with Scorpio. Whether it's a party, creative project, or charity event, your Scorpio friend will want to take the reins. While she's not as obvious a leader as Aries or Capricorn, she knows how to get a job done. Her innate intensity means she doesn't do things in half measures, and must cross every *t* and dot every *i* before she signs off on anything. In fact, Scorpio is secretly a control freak; she needs to be in control of a situation in order to feel comfortable. Leaving someone else to handle the details makes her feel as though she's letting someone else run her life—and no one tells Scorpio what to do. So when your scorpion friend pulls a power trip the next time you're planning a night out, understand that power and control make her feel safe.

It's Scorpio's desire for safety that also prompts her need for privacy. Difficult to get to know at first, Scorpio plays her cards close to her chest, and reveals herself fully to only a chosen few. Don't be surprised if years go by before you know details about her childhood—or even what her favorite food is. All of this secrecy is because Scorpio believes deep down that she is better off alone. She has trouble with trusting others, which explains her inability to express what she is feeling, in fear that it will be used against her. If your Scorpio friend gives you space, understand that she means no harm; it's just who she is.

However, once Scorpio deems you trustworthy, she'll show you a sense of loyalty like no other. Her allegiance is so intense that she might even come across as jealous or possessive when you mention hanging out with other friends. Though the scorpion has a steely exterior, still waters run deep—which is not surprising considering she is a water sign. Emotions can overcome her like a tidal wave, especially where her loved ones are involved. While you might feel like your Scorpio friend is too overprotective at times, it's important to know her devotion comes from deep appreciation. Scorpio doesn't do casual friends or acquaintances: once she's in, she's all in.

The Mysterious One: Where You'll Meet Scorpio

Scorpio is a natural introvert, so she doesn't usually choose to be around people, let alone large groups of people, for fun. Instead, she likes to cultivate her hobbies behind closed doors. However, she does enjoy activities that connect her to the core of who she is, including meditation and writing classes. Artistic endeavors that require detail and concentration, like ballroom dancing, jewelry making, and knitting, are also up Scorpio's alley.

Because she rules birth and death, you can also find Scorpio leading a birthing class, working as a mortician, or reading your tarot cards. No matter where you meet Scorpio, you'll recognize her by her quiet intensity. She pours herself into whatever she does, always ensuring her work is top-notch, which will undoubtedly cause you to give her a second look.

Going Deep: How to Become Friends with Scorpio

Scorpio is not for the faint of heart. She is the quintessential strong-but-silent type, and can be very intimidating. While Scorpio is aloof and mysterious, she also craves connection. She has killer instincts, and knows intuitively whether or not you'll be a good fit for her tribe—without you even saying a word. So don't be surprised if she silently sidles up to you first. However, if you are brave enough to strike up a conversation with Scorpio, don't be afraid to be completely yourself. She appreciates authenticity and always knows when someone's faking it, so you might as well be yourself. Delve deep into who you are and what you think and why, and you'll pique Scorpio's curiosity; venture into dark territory, such as death or the occult, and you'll win her admiration. While she might take time warming up to you, know that once she puts you in her contacts list, you're golden.

Inauthentic Ignoramus: Scorpio Friendship Dislikes

Because it takes so long for Scorpio to open up to her friends, trust is everything to her. Scorpio's dedication to living her life as truthfully as possible means untrustworthy friends need not apply. She is never anyone else but her true self, so she must feel she can act and express this self in front of her friends without being judged or critiqued for it. This also includes having friends who can create a safe zone to help her reveal her secrets and the depths of her soul. This is why if Scorpio considers you a friend, she wants to open up to you—and wishes for you to do the same.

Scorpio's desire—nay, *need*—for deep discussions are integral to her friendships. She needs to express her thoughts on anything and everything—and the deeper the topic, the better. If you can't keep up with highly evolved talks about the unknown and what it means to be human, well, you'll be shown the door. Betray her trust, and you will also have an enemy for life.

Stinging Like a Scorpion: How Scorpio Handles Conflict

For starters, you don't want to make waves with Scorpio. Like her symbol, the scorpion, your Scorpio friend is not one to be underestimated, and will sting her enemies if provoked. If she feels just the tiniest bit of injustice or injury, be prepared for a world-class smackdown; you will be in for a barrage of biting comments. Like everything else in her life, it's all or nothing when it comes to arguments, and Scorpio is quick to burn bridges. Doing her wrong in any capacity is viewed by Scorpio as a betrayal, and nothing hits her harder than a breach of trust. This is why she has no issue turning her back on you for good.

The best way to smooth things over with Scorpio is to not counterattack. Poking the bear—or in this case, the scorpion—will only make things worse. Let Scorpio say what she needs to say, and, if you can, let it go. It doesn't mean you think what she said is right, but moving on is the quickest way to diffuse Scorpio's temper. While her knee-jerk reaction is an effort to push you away no matter how big or small the argument was, if you believe in the sanctity of your friendship, try wrapping your Scorpio friend up in a big bear hug. It will help melt the armor around her heart, relinquish her stinger, and rid her of her hubris.

Light and Love: Maintaining Your Friendship with Scorpio

Your Scorpio friend might hide her vulnerability, but don't kid yourself: she feels a lot. Despite her cool and composed outer shell, she yearns to expose all of her deepest feelings to someone she trusts. Being patient, while also providing a safe space for your Scorpio friend to share her innermost thoughts, is one of the best gifts you can give her. While it might take a while for her to open up, knowing she is welcomed to will mean so much to her.

Whether or not she cares to admit it, your dark and deep Scorpio pal also needs a little light in her life. Encourage her to take things less seriously by awakening her sardonic sense of humor and helping her get out of her own head. Suggest a night of dancing or attending an upbeat concert. While she might not seem outwardly responsive to optimism, she'll truly appreciate the effort (and will enjoy it despite herself).

Scorpio is also a sensitive and loyal creature. She doesn't like feeling taken for granted or being ignored, so sending a "How are you?" text message or including her in group outings—even if she doesn't actually go—will mean a lot to your Scorpio friend. Knowing you think of her warms her seemingly black heart. She also longs to be understood and accepted for who she is. She knows she's a bit eccentric and that she can be a lot to take at times. However, her fear is that the very things that make her who she is will be the same things that push people away. While she is a natural loner, she does crave company and unconditional love. Expressing how much you wholly appreciate your Scorpio friend, including taking an interest in her hobbies, will mean everything to her.

BFF Bonus Points

Scorpio likes gifts that help her feel something, like vinyl records of her favorite moody music or a framed personal photograph. Because the bedroom is her favorite room in the house, gifting her with satin sheets, cozy throw blankets, or even a sexy pair of pajamas will also do.

Friendship Sign Compatibility

Is a friendship between Scorpio and Aquarius destined for failure? What makes Capricorn a good fit for this mysterious water sign. In the following section, you'll discover each of Scorpio's friendship matches, as well as how she operates in her connections with signs that aren't listed as her top matches.

Scorpio and Aries

These signs share a bold intensity for life; however, they channel it in different ways, which might make it difficult to form a true connection. Aries charges ahead—*using* his head—while Scorpio's more smoldering drive comes from her heart. It's hard for them to see eye to eye at times, and there may be power struggles at play. While the ram is quick to shrug off an argument, the scorpion will hold a grudge. However, if they're able to make use of their passionate natures via a project or charity work, this friendship can work.

Scorpio and Taurus

The scorpion and the bull might be astrological opposites, but a great friendship can lie underneath all the complexity. Scorpio and Taurus are concerned with practical matters, and both also share an excellent sense of humor, which eases up any sense of awkwardness. And, yes, there can be awkwardness—particularly when the bull is dismissive of the scorpion's emotions, and the scorpion labels the bull "lazy." They may be stubborn, but they can make their friendship work if they accept each other for who they are.

Scorpio and Gemini

This friendship embodies extreme energies—the still Scorpio versus the frenetic Gemini—which is why it might be difficult for these signs to find common ground. Gemini likes to encourage change, while Scorpio prefers stability. Oftentimes Gemini disappears to play with his other friends and Scorpio is left alone, brooding. However, the scorpion admires the agile mind of the twin, while the twin appreciates the scorpion's deep-rooted thinking. If these two can learn to accept their differences and bond over their mutual love for challenges, like board games and puzzles, they can salvage this connection.

Scorpio and Cancer

When two water signs come together, you can expect a ton of waterworks. Because both Scorpio and Cancer deal with life through an emotional lens, they will feel more comfortable sharing their innermost secrets and emotions with each other than with other signs. The scorpion is fond of the crab's nurturing ways (and home-cooked meals), and the crab values the scorpion's ability to understand and appreciate her for who she is. Both fans of water sports and creative activities, there's never a dull moment between these two.

Scorpio and Leo

Try as they might to get along, these two signs may keep hitting a wall whenever they hang out together. The loud lion can be too overwhelming for the introverted scorpion. Also, Leo's full social calendar may cause Scorpio to feel left out a lot. Tack on the fact that both stubborn signs prefer to be in charge of situations and insist on being right all the time, and there's no wonder a great deal of friction will exist between them. Accepting each other's differences will help this friendship last.

Scorpio and Virgo

A meeting of the minds occurs whenever Scorpio and Virgo are together. Both signs appreciate deep, philosophical discussions, as well as quiet nights in watching movies or playing board games. The scorpion appreciates the virgin's practical insight on life, and the virgin admires the scorpion's passion for life. While Virgo's meticulousness may annoy Scorpio, and Virgo may find Scorpio's moodiness frustrating, this friendship can be rewarding for both.

When Stars Align

Virgo adds structure to Scorpio's life. She shouldn't be afraid to share practical advice with her scorpion friend, especially when it comes to setting boundaries for Scorpio's emotional nature.

Scorpio and Libra

These signs intrigue each other. Scorpio admires Libra's ease with people, while Libra is fascinated by Scorpio's unconventional approach to life. When it comes to getting things done, like a special event, this is a great astrological combo. Libra, the cardinal sign, will get the planning started, while Scorpio, the fixed sign, will see it through. However, the flightiness of the scales may irritate the scorpion from time to time, and the scorpion's brooding may confuse the lighthearted scales.

Scorpio and Scorpio

Two scorpions together create an intense friendship that is mercurial to say the least. While these signs certainly understand each other almost telepathically, their touchy and sensitive natures may mean jealousy and possessiveness are regular players in their friendship. Their mutual passions will ignite creative projects, but also result in numerous blowups that run the risk of permanently damaging their relationship. Each should practice giving into the other in order for this friendship to last.

Scorpio and Sagittarius

When moody Scorpio needs a change of scenery, she will call her adventurous Sagittarius friend. The scorpion admires the archer's passion for exploration, from his globe-trotting tendencies to his philosophical inclinations, and knows she can always count on him for a little perspective. Sagittarius appreciates Scorpio's follow-through, so whenever he has the urge to flit from adventure to adventure, he knows Scorpio's dedication will help make things happen. However, Scorpio may find Sagittarius to be too chatty and unreliable at times. Likewise, Sagittarius may think Scorpio's secretive and aloof nature creates a dissonance. This connection works best where travel is concerned.

Scorpio and Capricorn

These two signs make a powerful connection, despite their obvious differences. Scorpio's emotional nature helps Capricorn connect to her own feelings, while Capricorn's stability helps Scorpio feel secure. Both signs are ambitious, hardworking, and responsible, which makes working on projects together a breeze. While Scorpio might find Capricorn bossy and Capricorn may be irritated by Scorpio's moodiness, these deep signs have enough in common to experience a long-lasting friendship.

When Stars Align

It's easy for Capricorn to become even more serious with deep Scorpio. She should remember to inject humor into a conversation to lighten the mood. Scorpion's trademark sarcasm will appreciate it.

Scorpio and Aquarius

Scorpio can't quite figure out Aquarius, which says a lot. The scorpion is confused by the water bearer's deep need for independence and cavalier attitude toward friendship. Aquarius, on the other hand, doesn't understand Scorpio's jealous streak or desire to stay inside when there are things to do outside. While Scorpio finds Aquarius's philosophy on life to be refreshing and Aquarius admires Scorpio's depth, these two will need to communicate well or else will find themselves on a sinking ship.

Scorpio and Pisces

The go-getter meets her perfect cheerleader when these signs unite. Scorpio's strength and decisiveness is a great match for the dreamy and indecisive Pisces, while Pisces's creativity inspires Scorpio. These two can make anything fun, and they will especially enjoy themselves when partaking in water activities together or discussing spiritual topics. Factor in their strong intuitions and these two are a dynamite combination.

Friendship Planets: Venus and Jupiter

To get the full scope of your friendship personalities, as well as how they work together, look at where the planets of Venus and Jupiter fall in your friend's and your charts, in addition to your Sun signs. The sensual planet Venus rules love and unions of all kinds, including your relationships with your friends. It indicates *how* you love others. Jupiter, meanwhile, indicates how you *show* your love. The planet of optimism, success, and generosity, its influence nudges you to open yourself up to new experiences and friendships.

Venus in Scorpio

Venus in Scorpio is a hard nut to crack. As she is cool at first, most people have a hard time figuring her out. That's fine by her, because she's highly selective when it comes to who she allows into her crew; she has zero time for flaky or fake friends. It's only once she implicitly trusts someone that she shows how much she really cares. And she cares a lot. Venus in Scorpio will go above and beyond for her friendships, staying up until to three a.m. to talk through a personal crisis, offering her keen and profound insight. It is through this powerful intuition, in fact, that she can read her friends exceptionally well. She will reach out to them, offering encouragement and support before they even speak a word about their troubles.

Intensely loyal, Venus in Scorpio is a fierce friend who believes in long-term connections and keeping a strong hold on her inner circle—which is why she also has a jealous and possessive streak. While she has the best of intentions, her intensity can be off-putting for some. She should remember to give her friends some breathing room. It also bodes well for her to remember that she is well liked for who she is; she doesn't have to try as hard as she often does.

Jupiter in Scorpio

Jupiter in Scorpio possesses a magnetic, intense, and powerful presence. She is a passionate person who prefers to dig deep rather than skate on the surface of life. She helps remind her friends of their innermost desires, and her relentless drive and focus shows others that anything is possible if you put everything you've got into your goals.

Being the emotional and empathetic creature that she is, Jupiter in Scorpio values intimacy and bases her friendships on whether she feels comfortable enough to be vulnerable with them. Her deep well of emotions encourages her loved ones to get in touch with their own emotions. She prefers having these deep discussions, in fact, that include expressing feelings with her friends, and believes these experiences create a stronger bond than superficial chitchat does. The downside of her living her emotional truth 24/7 is that she runs the risk of overwhelming others. Some people just don't have access to their emotions like she does, and realizing she can't change or mold people to how she sees fit is one of her biggest life lessons. If she can resist smothering her friends, she is sure to have a strong circle surrounding her for the rest of her days.

Chapter 9

Sagittarius
(November 22–December 21)

Once you converse with the chatty and laugh-out-loud funny Sagittarius for a few minutes, you'll discover why he is the most likeable, exciting person you will ever meet. With the king-sized planet Jupiter as his ruler, Sagittarius lives life to the fullest, and will inspire you to do the same.

The Explorer

Sagittarius is always aiming for the stars. He is on a constant journey, both mentally and physically—after all, symbolized by the archer-centaur, he is always directing his attention to one lofty goal after the other (and he rarely misses his mark). The symbolism is actually twofold for this sign, as the centaur, a half-human half-horse creature, reflects the human qualities of intellect and philosophical pursuits blending with the wild animal's inherent desire to be free and roam the earth as it pleases. It is no surprise then that your Sagittarius friend has a sharp inquiring mind and is constantly on the search for wisdom—wherever it takes him. This is why your Sagittarius friend likes to engage in deep discussions on theology and various viewpoints, and also craves a deeper connection with his inner circle. He will probe you on the inner workings of your life because he wants to get to know you inside and out.

His exploring mind translates to his outer world too. As a fire sign, he is enthusiastic about life, and needs to be in constant contact with the world to experience it as much as possible. Simply, Sagittarius cannot be confined: his adventurous and restless spirit thrives on change. Nine-to-five jobs don't work for Sagittarius; he wants a life of freedom that takes him around the world. He is inspired by travel and excitement, and is always on the lookout for something new to discover. His ease with taking risks and making big leaps also means he loves pushing his friends to explore their own senses of adventure. Your Sagittarius friend is the first person to suggest going away on vacation, camping, or exploring new sights in your hometown—anything that reeks of newness and utter delight. While his commitment to a fast-moving and unconventional lifestyle can be overwhelming at times—especially for those who prefer coloring within the lines—it's hard to deny that he instills a sense of possibility that is both infectious and inspiring. No doubt your world will be expanded thanks to Sagittarius.

Written in the Stars

Sagittarius just wants to have fun. Your Sagittarius friend is open to having adventures of any sort—whether that means taking an impromptu road trip or vacation, or doing something completely out of the ordinary, like a scavenger hunt. Throw out the itinerary and go where the wind takes you.

The Optimist

"The sun will come out tomorrow" is the best adage to sum up your Sagittarius buddy. As a passionate and effervescent fire sign, he is blessed with a cheerful disposition that always sees the glass as half full. No matter what life throws at him, he is never down for too long.

Sagittarius is also a mutable sign, meaning he was born during the transition from one season (fall) to the next (winter). As such, Sagittarius knows how to go with the flow. Easygoing and resilient, he instinctively understands how to make lemonade out of lemons. His happy-go-lucky and can-do attitude is the perfect antidote to your own blue mood. Whenever you're feeling down, your Sagittarius friend will do everything he can to help lift your spirits. He'll send you a funny GIF, put on your favorite movie, or order your go-to comfort food. Even while you are in the depths of despair, Sagittarius will make you see and believe there is a light at the end of the tunnel. And he will often pull a laugh out of you in the process.

Blessed with a great sense of humor, your Sagittarius friend loves making people laugh, in fact. As a gifted conversationalist with a playful spirit, he has a knack for entertaining people. He is the ideal person to inject a much-needed dosage of fun in a dull day or event. His contagious positive energy will help you believe that life is truly beautiful—or at least more manageable.

Sagittarius Quirks: The Autonomous Archer

Your Sagittarius friend is the quintessential free spirit. Prone to boredom, he has a fierce independence that allows him to explore and investigate his interests solo; he doesn't require a friend to accompany him on his journey, and he certainly doesn't need, or want, anyone's permission to follow his heart's desires. No one tells Sagittarius how to live. He will happily travel around the world, move cross-country, accept a lower-paying wage, or do whatever else it takes to be freely himself and to live the life he wants, on his terms. For those who find themselves bored or trapped by their daily routines, Sagittarius will help liberate them from their doldrums and remind them what it feels like when they get to do what they really want to do. His specialties include spontaneous road trips and keeping you up way past your bedtime, doing whatever strikes your fancy. However, with your Sagittarius friend's quest for freedom comes a price: he doesn't like anything or anyone interfering with what he sets out to achieve. The archer can thus be aloof and difficult to get a hold of, especially when he's in the midst of, or in search of, his next adventure.

As a result of his expeditions, he often has many friends, and flits from group to group. He tends to focus on friends who exist in his current daily life, and has trouble keeping in contact with friends from the past. It's nothing personal; it's just a result of Sagittarius being more concerned with what's around the corner than what is in the past. You'll also find that your Sagittarius friend often skates on the surface of life, and has trouble when things get messy or overly emotional. He doesn't have time for drama; he's got things to do. While his jam-packed schedule might make the archer come across as flaky and forgetful, he tries to make every moment count when he does see you—even if it's for a quick catch-up session. Also, because he enjoys his space, you can count on the fact that Sagittarius will always give you yours, and is never possessive or jealous when you're busy with other friends.

Brash and Braggy

The (aptly named) archer is a straight shooter, to say the least. He won't hesitate to tell you how it is, and always speaks his mind no matter what the consequences may be. Sagittarius is quick to overstep boundaries in the name of the whole truth and nothing but the truth. And while he might say what you need to hear, from needing to dump your partner to needing to dump your wardrobe, his delivery can often come across as tactless and even hurtful. Not surprisingly, he is often a victim of "foot in mouth" syndrome and must learn that he shouldn't always say whatever he wants to say, whenever he wants to say it. On the flip side, your Sagittarius pal will say the things you're too scared to voice yourself. If someone verbally attacks you, or if you find yourself in an uncomfortable position, the archer will step up to the plate to defend you.

Sagittarius's exuberance for life, not to mention his love for an audience, can also easily spin a story into a good (and embellished) yarn. Sagittarius loves to talk, especially about himself, to the point where his unbridled enthusiasm can border on self-indulgence and boastfulness. Part of being an energetic (yet also impulsive) fire sign means a tendency to be bossy and selfish, which can sum up your Sagittarius friend in his less-favorable moments.

Since the archer is so worldly and intelligent, he loves inspiring and educating others through his words and experiences, including his many achievements. But as the self-assured and confident creature that he is, his advice can often come across as preachy and overbearing. Sagittarius is also quick to become argumentative when someone doesn't see eye to eye with him, or when he doesn't get his own way. However, since he's also a mutable sign, he can easily bounce back from a difference of opinion and is adept at quickly redirecting a heated conversation back to pleasantries. Ultimately, as one of the most agreeable and charming signs in the zodiac, Sagittarius's big mouth can be one of his most endearing qualities—or a quirk that you accept as part of his larger-than-life personality.

The Adventurer: Where You'll Meet Sagittarius

Because of his adventurous spirit and love for travel, you'll most likely meet Sagittarius while on vacation. However, with such a wide array of interests and a high energy, the chances of meeting Sagittarius anywhere are pretty great. Due to his desire for change and freedom, Sagittarius is drawn to entrepreneurship, as well as positions that keep him busy and on the road, like pilot, salesperson, or social media influencer. The archer loves making people think and laugh, especially in front of an audience, so you may also find him in a writing group, comedy troupe, or theater class. His high energy and love for the outdoors can also mean that you meet him while cycling, hiking, or horseback riding (Sagittarius is part horse, after all). As a huge animal lover, he can also be found at a dog park, cat café, or animal shelter.

You'll recognize Sagittarius by his friendly, feisty, and outgoing nature, as well as his constant need for movement and stimulation. He is the one who can't sit still, and who doesn't like being told what to do, yet manages to have everyone eating out of the palm of his hand.

Written in the Stars
As a constant jetsetter, Sagittarius longs for exotic adventures, the further away from home, the better. Rio de Janeiro, Istanbul, and Thailand are all on his list. The best part of going on an excursion with the archer? As an experienced traveler, he knows all of the best travel hacks.

Chatting 'Em Up and Making 'Em Chuckle: How to Become Friends with Sagittarius

It's not difficult to befriend Sagittarius. He's interested in talking to anyone about anything, especially topics that intrigue him the most. Chat him up on politics, pop culture, or his latest adventure, and you'll quickly win him over. As the risk-taker he is, Sagittarius also appreciates those who are bold and don't mind stirring the pot a bit. The archer loves being challenged, so starting a lively debate or inviting him to a thought-provoking game, like trivia or poker, is a great way to earn your way into his good graces. Tickling Sagittarius's funny bone will also win you major bonus points with this amateur comedian. A word to the wise, though: stay away from getting too deep and personal too soon, or you might scare him away. Reveal yourself to be intelligent and brave, with a good sense of humor, and you'll hit the bull's-eye in this friendship.

Neediness and Needless Drama: Sagittarius Friendship Dislikes

Sagittarius doesn't do needy or clingy; he won't take kindly to anyone who impedes upon his freedom. Constant texting or demands for his time will not go over well. Prying into his personal business too soon or without him offering the information himself is another turnoff. Generally, the archer likes to keep things light until he gets to know and trust someone. If you bring down what was supposed to be a fun-loving time with drama or tears, it will be more than enough for him to say, "Sayonara."

Unfiltered and Unifying: How Sagittarius Handles Conflict

Sagittarius is an energetic, happy-go-lucky sign who prefers keeping his world as light and carefree as possible. Serious situations make him extremely uncomfortable, so he would rather sweep any sort of argument or conflict underneath the proverbial carpet than deal with it head-on. He hopes that if he doesn't bring it up, and ignores it for a while, meaning, like, forever, then it will just disappear, and you can return to being bosom buddies. However, once provoked, Sagittarius's sharp tongue has no choice but to come out. He will speak his mind no matter what, even if that means cutting you down to size just for the sake of "winning" the argument.

While he is known for easily walking away from situations and people, especially those he deems as high-maintenance and not worthy of his time, he would prefer to make amends as soon as possible. After all, he is more about keeping life fun than participating in things that only drag down the energy. He is usually the first to message, "But we're still cool, right?" after a showdown. If you can forgive Sagittarius for his unfiltered sparring and come to an agreement, your friendship has the chance to become stronger than ever. Just don't bring up the fight again; he hates reliving the past.

Space and Support: Maintaining Your Friendship with Sagittarius

Giving your Sagittarius friend a ton of space is one of the best things you can do. His freedom and independence are worth everything to him, and understanding and accepting that about him will do wonders for your friendship, both for Sagittarius's sake and your own. Know that it isn't personal when he doesn't call or text you back—he's probably just on another adventure. He'll call when he can. And, with so many places to go and people to see, the archer can be just plain forgetful when it comes to these things. While it's easy to become annoyed, acknowledging his absentmindedness as part of his nature, and valuing the time you do spend together, will go a long way in cementing your friendship.

Additionally, while your Sagittarius friend doesn't express his grouchy side often, he is prone to becoming touchy when he feels misunderstood for the choices he's made, especially those that are outside of the norm. This is why outwardly supporting his unconventional lifestyle will mean the world to Sagittarius; even texting a simple "You're awesome!" message will make his day.

For all his grandiose ideas, Sagittarius also has a tendency to procrastinate or bow out of a task altogether. Gently nudging him to follow through on an idea, while still encouraging his smarts and skills, will help boost his confidence and let him know you're on his side.

Friendship Signs Compatibility

What makes Sagittarius and Aries such a great duo? How might the adventurous Sagittarius and the homebody Cancer form a lasting bond? The following section details each of Sagittarius's ideal friendship matches, as well as how he operates in a relationship with a sign that isn't included in this list of compatible Sun signs.

Sagittarius and Aries

Sagittarius brings the chips and Aries brings the salsa to this complementary combo. Both trailblazers with boundless energy, these two definitely know how to play well together, whether it's enjoying a fitness class or painting the town red. Sagittarius appreciates Aries's can-do attitude, and Aries values Sagittarius's risk-taking instincts. Both power hungry, these two might bicker over who takes the lead; however, they forgive and forget easily, and will be onto the next adventure before they know it.

Sagittarius and Taurus

While these two like to eat good food and indulge in their latest whims together (especially those involving the outdoors), their similarities may end there. Sagittarius's wanderlust can be too overwhelming and unsettling for grounded Taurus, while Taurus's homebody tendencies may bore and irritate Sagittarius. However, the flexibility of Sagittarius bodes well with Taurus's innate stubbornness, as Sagittarius can easily go along with whatever Taurus wants to do.

Sagittarius and Gemini

Sagittarius and Gemini are astrological opposites, but in this instance, opposites definitely attract. These two can stay up late discussing deep issues like philosophy and politics, and are also just as comfortable exploring museums and art galleries together. The twin easily gives the space that the archer needs, while the archer doesn't mind the twin's frenetic energy. Though Sagittarius may get annoyed at Gemini for canceling plans at the last minute, and Gemini dislikes Sagittarius's bluntness, these two make great friends.

When Stars Align
It's important in this friendship for Gemini to cool it with his verbal teasing. Sagittarius can dish it out, but he often can't take it.

Sagittarius and Cancer

Sagittarius is the constant explorer; Cancer is the consummate homemaker. The archer lives for change, while the crab thrives on comfort. These two signs couldn't be more different at first glance, but there's a lot to be learned from each other if given the chance. Sagittarius can add diversity to Cancer's routine, and Cancer offers Sagittarius the stability and emotional support he may not realize he needs sometimes. Together they can make each other LOL and will bond over their shared love for movies and food.

Sagittarius and Leo

Look out: Sagittarius and Leo are quite an exciting pair. Both are intelligent and vibrant signs with a penchant for adventure, the spotlight, and practical jokes. This is a fun-loving friendship full of vacations and hitting up the latest hot spots in town. The archer appreciates the lion's big heart, and the lion adores the archer's passion for life. While they might fight for control at times, these two ultimately respect each other enough to let bygones be bygones, quickly moving onto the next fun experience.

Sagittarius and Virgo

Though these two have the best of intentions, sometimes it's hard for Sagittarius and Virgo to see eye to eye. Sagittarius's freewheeling lifestyle upsets Virgo's carefully constructed world. Conversely, Virgo's cautious and perfectionist nature can be too much to bear for spontaneous Sagittarius. Sagittarius's preachy ways are also a point of contention for Virgo, who is too reserved for passionate Sagittarius. However, both signs are very direct with what they want, and if Sagittarius can help Virgo lighten up, and Virgo can provide safety for Sagittarius, this friendship can last.

Sagittarius and Libra

These social butterflies love meeting new people and trying new experiences together. Sagittarius and Libra never run out of things to say to each other, and their keen minds always keep the conversations stimulating. Their road trips are always memorable, and Libra's diplomacy makes it easier for Sagittarius to take the lead. While the scales' indecisiveness irritates the archer, and the archer's bluntness gets on the scales' nerves, these will have many road trips together—as long as they focus on the joy they bring to each other's lives.

Sagittarius and Scorpio

Both stubborn and strong personalities, Sagittarius and Scorpio are a difficult match. Sagittarius is an open book (once you get to know him) who wants to explore the outside world, while Scorpio is closed off and prefers to explore her inner self. The archer may grow weary of the scorpion's moodiness, while the scorpion may be easily annoyed by the archer's sunny disposition. Given the chance (and a big dose of patience), however, Sagittarius can expand Scorpio's world, and Scorpio can help ground Sagittarius.

Sagittarius and Sagittarius

These two love each other. The archers appreciate each other's sense of adventure and upbeat personality. They make ideal travel companions, and are always up for the next fun thing to do on a Saturday night—or for just talking about the mysteries of life. While they lack boundaries and there's no voice of reason when they embark on potentially dangerous activities, they truly enjoy each other's company and their agreeable natures means fighting is a nonissue.

Sagittarius and Capricorn

Sagittarius is upbeat, whimsical, and spontaneous, while Capricorn is serious, practical, and even a little shy. While at first these signs might not seem to have a lot in common, if they take the time to get to know each other, they could develop a friendship that complements each of their unique personalities. They both adore traveling, and have a great sense of humor that can cement their bond. While Sagittarius might see Capricorn as a "Debbie Downer" at times, and Capricorn may think Sagittarius too self-indulgent, they have the ability to work out any minor bumps to enjoy a smooth friendship.

Sagittarius and Aquarius

Both adventurous and independent signs, these two march to the beat of their own drums, and it's the other's uniqueness that each digs about the other. Both Sagittarius and Aquarius will love discussing deep things together, and they will feel connected on a soul level through these conversations. Together they can push each other to explore even further, and support each other when things don't go exactly as planned. Their minimal differences are easy to ignore when they feel so at peace and at home with each other.

Sagittarius and Pisces

Independent Sagittarius may feel smothered by emotional Pisces, and demure Pisces may feel insecure around bold Sagittarius. The fish needs stability and support, while the archer is all about change and freedom. Sagittarius's brutal honesty may also offend and hurt the sensitive Pisces, while Pisces's mood swings may drive Sagittarius away. If both signs can focus on their mutual spirituality and love for discussing life's biggest questions, as well as their interest in water sports, they can avoid drowning their connection.

When Stars Align
Pisces should send a "How are you feeling today?" text to her Sagittarius friend every once in a while. Sagittarius often neglects to check in with his feelings, so he appreciates Pisces's empathetic nature.

Friendship Planets: Venus and Jupiter

Considering the planets of Venus and Jupiter in your friend's and your charts, in addition to the Sun signs, can help you gain a better understanding of your friend and your friendship with them. Venus rules love and unions of all kinds, including your relationships with your friends. It indicates *how* you love. The planet of optimism, success, and generosity, Jupiter indicates how you *show* your love. Its influence nudges you to experience new things in life, and shows how outgoing, friendly, and generous you are with others.

Venus in Sagittarius

Venus in Sagittarius is an upbeat, candid free spirit who has a large of collection of friends from his various travels and adventures. Not one for seriousness—he pretty much runs away from the slightest whiff of emotional drama—he prefers his friendships to be light and fun. Quick to crack a joke and always up for a good time, Venus in Sagittarius's exuberant vibes attract people to him. He makes even the most mundane experience something joyful and worth remembering. He likes friends who can keep up with his high energy and who want to explore life, both figuratively and literally, as much as he does.

Venus in Sagittarius loves helping his nearest and dearest to broaden their horizons, whether through traveling or discussing life's deepest mysteries. His commitment to living life on his terms is inspiring to his friends, and it pushes them to search for and experience more themselves. However, because he has a myriad of interests, as well as a fear of being still for too long, it's difficult for him to keep in touch regularly with his friends, which might irritate some. It would serve Venus in Sagittarius to be more mindful of his friends' feelings; letting them know he is thinking of them despite his busy schedule will go a long way.

Jupiter in Sagittarius

Jupiter in Sagittarius is an outgoing, powerful, and positive thinker who's dedicated to making his wildest dreams come true—both for himself and for his loved ones. He encourages his friends to explore new horizons, whether that means suggesting that they immerse themselves in new cities and cultures, or helping them open their minds and hearts to create more fulfillment and live their best lives. His need for constant growth and change is inspiring for his friends, and he takes great pride whenever they take risks in their lives, because he knows that leaps of faith have a way of paying off (and he can't help but feel like he's played a small part in their success).

Jupiter in Sagittarius's enthusiasm for life is infectious, which is why he is the first person his friends turn to whenever they're having a bad day or feeling defeated. Blessed with an optimistic countenance, he instantly knows how to cheer someone up and point them in the right direction. However, as knowledgeable as he is, he should be careful that his advice doesn't come across as self-righteous or condescending. Additionally, while his pioneering spirit is motivating, it would bode well for him to stay grounded at times and appreciate the present moment with his friends, rather than focusing on the next adventure. After all, the here and now often provides the biggest lessons, and life feels all the sweeter when you see it as a journey rather than a destination.

Chapter 10

Capricorn
(December 22–January 19)

Symbolized by the sea goat, there are two sides to Capricorn. The first side (the mountain goat) represents her ambitious take-charge nature, while the other side (the fish) represents a sensitivity lurking beneath the surface. While her stoic nature can be off-putting at times, your Capricorn friend is privately an emotional person whom you can always rely on for support.

The Organizer

At the heart of Capricorn is her resolute astuteness and dedication to getting things done. After all, her ruling planet is Saturn, which bestows organization, structure, and discipline. This explains why Capricorn is one of your most hardworking friends, and why she will always stick to her word and arrive to an event on time (or early). Fulfilling obligations, planning things out, and taking personal responsibility are very important to Capricorn. According to Roman mythology, Saturn was also the father to many other gods, which can explain Capricorn's tendency to take on a "parental" role in her friendships.

Since she's also a cardinal sign—which bestows ambition and initiation—your Capricorn friend naturally takes on the leadership role in your friendship. She actually enjoys managing projects and people, so it comes as no surprise that she's the friend who initiates planning and organizing getaways, parties, and reunions. Her inherent dependable nature (which stems from her astrological element, earth) comes in handy when you need someone to look after your plants and pets while on vacation, or to remind you to pay your rent on time.

While her intense organizational skills hint that your Capricorn friend can be a perfectionist at times, she is far more likely to hold herself to impossible standards than she is others. So if you make a mistake or forget to follow through with a task, your sea goat pal will easily cut you some slack and help you out as best she can.

While Capricorn is also good at adapting to change, she prefers to stick to her routines and what she knows. She likes security, which explains why she can come across as controlling sometimes, especially when leading a project or an event. The sea goat doesn't like to leave anything to chance—and she can have a hard time trusting that someone else will complete a task as well as she does—so she often has a lot of pots on the stove with only one cook in the kitchen. However, if you find your Capricorn friend has taken on more than she can handle, gently remind her that it's okay to delegate. She'll relinquish the reins a little bit—enough to get some air and try again tomorrow.

The Family Friend

As a friend of Capricorn, rest assured that you are in fact adored by her, even if she doesn't say it. Capricorn takes most things seriously (she's a pretty serious person, after all) which means she takes her friendships seriously too. As her ruling planet, the patriarchal Saturn, suggests, Capricorn is a traditionalist at heart. Family means everything to her, and friends = family to Capricorn.

She is also extremely particular about whom she chooses as her friends. True, she can come across as picky when it comes to befriending new people, but that's because she easily picks up on the true intentions of others—and is usually right. To the mighty sea goat, quality trumps quantity, always. Her group of friends might be small, but that's simply because she abides by the adage "Mi casa es su casa." She needs to feel secure that you're willing to be a part of her family, because she has no problem including her tribe in family dinners, gatherings, and vacations. In fact, doing so feels natural for her. Not including a best friend in an intimate celebration, like her dad's retirement dinner, actually feels strange to Capricorn. She's also the friend who will remember every birthday with a thoughtful card and who will check in when you haven't touched base in a while. So when Capricorn tells you she thinks of you as family, believe it.

Capricorn Quirks: The Stubborn Sea Goat

Your Capricorn friend doesn't understand the meaning of FOMO (fear of missing out) because she is usually doing what she wants to do most: working. The ambitious sea goat can be so focused on her career and lofty aspirations, in fact, that she may neglect her friends. So when your Capricorn friend skips a night on the town with you, try not to take it personally. She is only doing what comes naturally to her. Cajoling her won't work either, thanks to her classic Capricorn stubbornness. It's no wonder she's often called rigid, and even referred to sometimes as a wet blanket; she has an inherent resistance to going with the flow. She doesn't like flow; she likes plans of action that go according to, well, plan. If anything is out of the ordinary or doesn't measure up to her high standards, it is likely to put her in a bad mood. Capricorn is the definition of a type A personality (and a control freak).

However, need help with a last-minute project, or inspiration to crack down on something you're procrastinating? Your Capricorn friend will be that person to either lend a hand or serve as the motivation to get things done. In fact, her friends may be intimidated by Capricorn's extreme work ethic and intense drive. Imagine being friends with Michelle Obama or Justin Trudeau (both Capricorns) and you may understand why it can be unsettling for some friends to be around such a fierce go-getter. However, if you can view her extreme work ethic as a means of inspiration, and understand that her commitment to her goals doesn't mean she doesn't value your friendship, you have a tremendous friend in Capricorn.

Sarcastic and Sensitive

For all of her serious ways, your Capricorn friend has a few fun tricks up her sleeve that make her all the more endearing. For starters, you'll love her wicked sense of humor. Yes, hidden underneath her reserved appearance lies a secret sharp sarcasm and dry wit unlike any other in the zodiac. You might not detect this at first, because Capricorn tends to save her funny streak for her tried and trusted tribe members. But once you make the cut, you'll know instantly whom to ask when you need a partner in crime to quietly heckle a boring networking event or make light of a heavy situation with a sarcastic comment. She's the one who will get you LOL-ing with an apropos GIF for your latest relationship drama, or send you into a fit of giggles by only using a single—yet hilarious—word or expression. You can be sure your inside jokes with Capricorn will have you laughing for years.

Yet it's Capricorn's vulnerability that is her most significant and surprising trait. She may not speak up often, but when she does, her words hold incredible weight. It's this often jarring vulnerability that allows her to connect so deeply and intensely with those close to her. It's also why you will always know where you stand with her. With Capricorn there are no games—

just truth. And when she gets emotional? Think Academy Award–winning tears. This is not because she is being dramatic—Capricorn is anything but—but because she seldom shows excessive feelings. So when she does, it is the result of these pent-up emotions. These are no crocodile tears, either—when Capricorn cries, it's always 100 percent real. Her emotional authenticity may even help you feel more comfortable with expressing and communicating your own feelings, which will strengthen your friendship. And since she's not a big talker, Capricorn relies on her actions to speak for themselves. Expect a care package when you're going through a bad breakup, or a generous gift certificate when you land your dream job; this is how she communicates her support and love for you.

Head of the Class: Where You'll Meet Capricorn

From the student council to the boardroom, chances are you'll meet your Capricorn friend where there's something to be achieved. Capricorn brings her ambitious and competitive spirit to every activity she does, including social ones. And while she is success-oriented, she's also the first to lend a helping hand and put the needs of others before her own. Because of this empathetic nature, you may also find her volunteering for a cause, like an animal shelter, or leading a project at a nonprofit organization. As an earth sign, Capricorn is also often drawn to outdoor activities that are steady and grounded, and which offer achievements she can strive for—like climbing to the top of a mountain, entering a marathon race, or backpacking to a hard-to-reach location.

Capricorn is easy to spot because she's the one in charge and with her head down doing the work, as opposed to the louder Aries leader. Instead of taking things on aggressively like the ram, Capricorn reacts quietly to situations and values the notion that success comes from continuous effort. It's her reserved but determined demeanour, along with her dry sense of humor, that will give Capricorn away to you.

Slow and Steady: How to Become Friends with Capricorn

At first approach, Capricorn is a lone wolf content in doing her own thing. She is polite and respectful, but she prefers not to get too close too soon. You might interpret her introversion for being cold or snobby, but she is really only being cautious and getting a better feel for her surroundings. So if you see a tenacious wallflower in your hot yoga class struggling to perfect every pose, you can bet she is a Capricorn. Don't be afraid to say hello, however; she doesn't bite. In fact, she will welcome the icebreaker. Following the introduction, be sure to stay persistent. Capricorn is hesitant to invest her time and energy into a new friend unless she gets the feeling that you are legitimate in your intentions. She values honesty and integrity. Reveal yourself to be a trustworthy friend with a good sense of humor, and you will make a friend for life in Capricorn.

Flakiness and Inauthenticity: Capricorn Friendship Dislikes

Capricorn may have the patience of a saint, but if it's constantly being pushed, she will give up on a friendship. She has zero time for flaky friends. She prefers those who are true to their word, who are punctual, and who understand that communication is vital to any relationship. She doesn't like to feel her time is being wasted or that she's not being valued. Seeing poor manners, being guilt-tripped into doing something she doesn't want to do, or catching even a whiff of inauthenticity is enough for Capricorn to unfriend you.

Verbal Sparring: How Capricorn Handles Conflict

Have an issue with your Capricorn friend? Be warned that you could be thrust into a vicious verbal duel. She is known for having a quick temper and being able to cut deeply using only words, thanks to her extensive vocabulary. She also has no problem with calling you out on any bad behavior, like a forgotten birthday or flippant remark, to ensure it won't happen again. Capricorn also turns to her trusted family members, including a wise parent or grandparent, for advice when handling conflict, which might irritate her friends. It's not that Capricorn can't fight her own battles—she certainly can—but she appreciates support and advice, and wants to learn from the past.

Though Capricorn is open to mature and grounded conversations in order to get to the root of an issue, she can be extremely stubborn, and has trouble owning up to her mistakes. When resolving any conflict, it's important for friends of Capricorn to give her time and space to process her feelings. And when it's time to communicate a problem, allow her the opportunity to explain her side of the issue without any interruption. Acknowledge your part and also voice an apology if necessary. Capricorn values truthful talks, as well as a solid heartfelt apology, and she is quick to forgive. But remember that Capricorn is true to her word. So if she says she is finished with you...? She means it.

Loyalty and Encouragement: Maintaining Your Friendship with Capricorn

Because your Capricorn friend tends to be a shy person and a bit of a loner, it's a good idea to encourage her to go out and let loose once in a while. Remind her that she's in safe company, and also let her know how much fun you think she is—because it's true. Once Capricorn lets down her hair, after all, she can actually be the life of the party. On the other hand, it's also important to be respectful of your Capricorn friend's need to be alone. She considers her private time to be sacred, so respecting her desire to fly solo will mean a lot to her. She'll know that you value her for being who she is.

Reminding your Capricorn friend to breathe is another kind gesture you can do for her. It's easy for the sea goat to become overwhelmed with the arduous tasks she gives herself, so having someone in her corner who can not only remind her to slow down but also remind her of the accomplishments she has already achieved goes a long way. Capricorn is often so focused on what she has yet to accomplish that she tends to forget how far she has actually come, so it's a nice idea to give her an encouraging pat on the back every once in a while. Even if she doesn't seem like she needs it, she will appreciate it.

Your Capricorn friend might not express sentimentality easily, but she is terrified you will forget her. This is why the *most* valuable gift that you can give her is your loyalty. Capricorn is one of the most, if not *the* most, fiercely loyal signs of the zodiac. There's nothing she wants more in the world in a friend than the assurance that you have her back and will stay loyal to her, no matter time or distance. Staying in touch, remembering her birthday, or texting her a quick message asking her how she is means everything to Capricorn.

Friendship Compatibility

Can Capricorn and Leo set aside their differences? What makes the bond between Capricorn and Taurus so rewarding? The following section sheds light on each of Capricorn's friendship matches, from the most compatible to the more challenging.

Capricorn and Aries

What do you get when you put the ambitious Capricorn together with the passionately driven Aries? Challenging teamwork. While both signs are very determined people, their approaches are opposite. The sea goat is patient and cool as a cucumber, while the ram is impulsive and hotheaded. However, there's a lot to be gained in this connection. Capricorn will admire Aries's enthusiasm, while Aries will benefit from Capricorn's calm and steadfast vibe. If they can learn to work through each other's differences, and focus on supporting each other's goals, this will be a winning friendship.

Capricorn and Taurus

Natural allies, these two feel very at home with each other. They enjoy talking about their wildest dreams together because they understand each other. Capricorn especially appreciates Taurus's loyalty and tenderness, while Taurus admires Capricorn's dependability and smart sense of humor. From staying at home watching movies to hitting up the newest restaurant, Capricorn and Taurus love spending time together no matter what they're doing.

When Stars Align
In need of a pick-me-up during a "blah" day at work? Capricorn is the best hilarious GIF-giver Taurus will ever meet.

Capricorn and Gemini

While on the surface Capricorn and Gemini are quite different signs, there's a lot to learn and enjoy in this connection. Gemini is flexible and relies on his quick wits to navigate life, while Capricorn is organized and relies on structure. However, the twin can draw the sea goat out of his strict shell, and the sea goat can provide grounding to the twin's chaotic energy. Most importantly, these two will crack each other up and can pass hours making each other laugh with funny web links and inside jokes.

Capricorn and Cancer

These signs are astrological opposites, and while there will be moments of tension between them, they can still develop a close friendship. Capricorn values Cancer's ability to make her feel at home, and Cancer admires Capricorn's steadfast ambition. However, the sea goat is easily annoyed by the crab's moodiness, and the crab doesn't care for the sea goat's seriousness. Luckily, their mutual love for shopping and fine food can save the day when tensions run high.

Capricorn and Leo

An unlikely duo, Capricorn and Leo can form a lasting friendship if they focus on appreciating each other instead of wishing the other were different. The lion can often steal the sea goat's thunder, while the sea goat's pragmatism can annoy the fun-loving lion. However, their shared ambition and desire for success can bond them for good—as long as their mutual opinionated natures don't drive them apart.

Capricorn and Virgo

This is a genuine connection. Although both cautious creatures, Capricorn and Virgo feel an immediate sense of comfort with each other. As earth signs, they view the world through a similar grounded and practical lens. From politics to pop culture, they can discuss anything because they both value and respect each other's opinions. They can easily talk for hours on end and it will feel like only minutes have passed. While the sea goat might grow weary of the virgin's impartiality, and the virgin might tire of the sea goat's need for control, this union has the markings of a lifelong friendship.

Capricorn and Libra

Try as they might, a friendship between these signs may have trouble taking off. Capricorn and Libra are inherently very different people. Libra is outgoing and loves having many friends, while Capricorn is reserved and prefers a smaller tribe. The sea goat is often irritated by the scales' indecisiveness, and the scales doesn't understand why the sea goat has to take life so seriously. However, because these two both aim for success and enjoy stimulating conversations, they could work well together on a creative project.

Capricorn and Scorpio

Quite simply, Capricorn and Scorpio are friends for life. Each appreciates the other's emotionally cautious nature, and they have a similarly sarcastic sense of humor. Together they share deep and meaningful conversations about everything from the professional to the profoundly personal. Even if the sea goat and the scorpion don't regularly talk as much as they'd like, they know that once they do get together, they can pick up right where they left off. And thanks to their shared respect for loyalty, they also know they have each other's backs.

Capricorn and Sagittarius

Capricorn and Sagittarius have a lot more in common than meets the eye. Both are intelligent and ambitious leaders who don't back away from a challenge. They also make each other laugh, and are amazing travel buddies. However, Capricorn may feel uncomfortable with Sagittarius's fickleness, while Sagittarius can be frustrated when Capricorn's stoicism replaces real emotions. Luckily, the archer can lighten up the serious sea goat, and the sea goat can ground the flighty archer. Ultimately, these two will need patience and communication in order to see eye to eye.

Capricorn and Capricorn

Sea goats respect each other. They know how hard they work, and they understand what it takes to stay organized and on top of their game no matter what life throws at them. Two Capricorns can make each other laugh like no other sign can, and they also appreciate each other's need to go home after they've had their fill of a party. However, two serious sea goats together mean it's difficult to lighten the vibe, and they could become too solemn for their own good. However, their shared loyalty means the world to them both.

Capricorn and Aquarius

On the surface, the straight-and-narrow Capricorn and the eccentric Aquarius might seem like total opposites, but they actually have the potential to form an unbreakable bond. Capricorn finds the free-spirited Aquarius to be a breath of fresh air, while Aquarius appreciates Capricorn's wise and practical demeanor (especially when in a jam). While Capricorn may tire of Aquarius's unpredictability, and Aquarius may think Capricorn can be a wet blanket at times, if they can value each other's differences, they will enjoy a unique connection. They will also need to ensure that their opinionated and implacable natures don't cause a rift.

Capricorn and Pisces

These two signs form a healing connection that can last through the ages. Capricorn is stable and grounded, which is exactly what the dreamy and emotional Pisces needs. The fish's vulnerability also gives the sea goat permission to openly express her feelings, which she appreciates. While Pisces's flightiness is enough to drive Capricorn batty, and Capricorn can be a little too pushy for Pisces, these signs feel safe and secure with each other. From watching rom-coms to working on creative projects together, they enjoy being in each other's company as often as they can.

Friendship Planets: Venus and Jupiter

To get the full scope of your friendship personalities, plus how well they may work together, look at the planets of Venus and Jupiter in both your friend's and your charts, in addition to your Sun signs. Venus rules love and unions of all kinds, including friendships. It indicates *how* you love. Jupiter, meanwhile, indicates how you *show* your love. The planet of optimism, success, and generosity, its influence nudges you to experience new things in life, and shows how outgoing, friendly, and generous you are with others, especially your friends.

Venus in Capricorn

Venus in Capricorn is cool, composed, and cautious. She prefers to size up her friends before she allows herself to truly let go and invite them into her inner circle. Once she does, however, she is loyal to a fault. Since she's so discriminating, those chosen to be tribe members understand the value of this decision. She also prefers to surround herself with responsible and dependable people—traits that she is also known to possess. Because loyalty and accountability are so important to her, she doesn't care for flaky or untrustworthy friends. When someone betrays her, it is gutting and can leave a mark for years.

While Venus in Capricorn is not outwardly affectionate with her friends, she feels quite deeply underneath. Friends are like family to her, and, like most things in her life, she takes her friendships very, very seriously. When it comes to showing her love, she prefers doing practical things for them. In fact, the category of love language that perfectly describes Venus in Capricorn is *acts of service*. From helping a friend move to sending recipes or useful interview tips that would be beneficial to a pal's career, she likes to help out as often as she can. Those closest to her also appreciate her quick-witted and dry sense of humor, and know they can rely on her for a laugh (especially in the midst of an awkward or dark situation). While she has a penchant to skip fun nights out in order to complete a work assignment, when she lets her hair down, she can light up the room.

Jupiter in Capricorn

Jupiter in Capricorn is responsible, with an old soul, and integrity means everything to her. A traditionalist, she prefers to make friends slowly and take her time before letting someone get to know her vulnerable side. She also likes to make plans about everything— whether it's something as extravagant as a thirtieth birthday party, or a simple Friday night out. Her word is worth its weight in gold, meaning once she says she'll do something or be somewhere, her friends can count on her to come through.

Tenacious and ambitious, Jupiter in Capricorn inspires friends with her persistence in overcoming any obstacle that life throws at her. They know that when she puts her mind to something, she'll get it done no matter what. Her ease with leadership coupled with her calm demeanor and rational mind are also gifts when it comes to dispensing advice or handling a crisis. When the chips are down, her tried and truest friends know whom to call in order to make it right. Her resourcefulness and pragmatism mean she can look at any situation or project and know what will work or won't work. And she likes to help out whenever she is needed; all her friends need to do is ask. Her aloof nature prevents her from intruding; however, it's important for her to realize that demonstrating her warm and affectionate side is a strength, not a weakness. She shouldn't let her innate pessimism win: she is always wanted and valued by her loved ones.

Chapter 11

Aquarius
(January 20–February 18)

Imaginative, innovative, and eccentric, Aquarius is a truth teller who wants to make the world a better place. He prefers to approach relationships with logic and reasoning, which is why he is able to visualize new possibilities and solutions: he doesn't let emotions cloud his thought process. No wonder your Aquarius friend is your go-to person when it comes solving any conflict.

The Humanitarian

If there was a motto that best summed up Aquarius it would be "We're all in this together." Ruled by Uranus, the planet of change, originality, and revolutionary vision, your Aquarius friend wants to make a solid difference in the world; couple this with his symbol, the water bearer, which carries water to the parched masses, and it is no wonder why your Aquarius pal is more concerned with what's best for everyone than with what is best for any one person, including himself. He believes in the strength of numbers and the power of friendships; he understands how intricately everyone is connected, and how relationships make the world go around. Aquarius believes you find meaning in your life through your friendships and the experiences you share with your friends, which is why he's always planning the next get-together (even before you've finished your current one). Open-minded and nonjudgmental, Aquarius is genuinely fascinated with people, and easily picks up allies from all walks of life wherever he goes. As an air sign, he has an endless curiosity about others and is adept at intellectualizing and seeing both sides of an argument, making him an excellent problem-solver.

While his collection of friends helps him understand and appreciate individual viewpoints, he tends to have more acquaintances than close pals. Though he *can* form deep bonds with friends, his innate distrust of emotions leads him to keep his squad at arm's length. However, there's no need to doubt your Aquarius friend's loyalty: as a fixed sign (born in the middle of the winter season)—which is characterized by stability and unwavering determination—he favors dependability and cherishes his friends more than anything in life. A true humanitarian, he isn't attached to possessions; he'll literally give you the shirt off his back if you admire it. Endlessly generous, he will do what he can to support you, from helping you write up a new resume to letting you borrow his car.

The Rebel

As friendly and considerate as Aquarius is, he's essentially a rebel at heart. He happily marches to the beat of his own drum and shuns any and all labels. You can't put Aquarius in a box—and he'll keep it that way, thank you very much. He frequently takes the road less traveled, and does the things that others might be scared to do. Your Aquarius friend is also allergic to boredom, and will do anything and everything in order to avoid it, which explains his jam-packed schedule. Inherently impulsive, thanks to his rebellious ruling planet, your water bearer pal is always down for something spontaneous and out of the ordinary. Unlike the adventurer Sagittarius, however, Aquarius wants ongoing mental stimulation; his fertile mind needs to be constantly fed with new people and experiences. He would play hooky from work to go visit a planetarium, for example.

Aquarius's unbridled bravery and passion for change can be inspiring and motivating to those who dream of doing bigger and better things with their lives. As the true maverick he is, when someone says, "This is how it's always been done," Aquarius will go out of his way to try things a different way. In fact, as an intellectual air sign, he's constantly thinking up new ways to do things. Thanks to his sharp mind and contrarian nature, the water bearer will always cross the finish line—especially if someone tells him it can't be accomplished. At the core of the renegade Aquarius is his desire to be free, especially to be himself, which is an inspiration for his friends to seek the same for themselves. If you're stumped on a project or can't seem to think outside of the box, reach out to your Aquarius friend for his advice: he'll know what to do. His rebellious nature also means he is prone to speak his mind at any given time, and has an acidic sense of humor that will both surprise and amuse you.

Aquarius Quirks: The Wacky Water Bearer

Your Aquarius friend is more than a little "out there." He's the edgy eccentric who is ahead of his time. And because he is the zodiac's futurist sign, he is naturally obsessed with technology (Have a tech issue? Consult Aquarius!), science fiction, and any sort of invention. Your Aquarius pal is the one who will line up for hours to get the newest smartphone, or drag you to the latest sci-fi blockbuster movie. Since he makes it a point to be at the forefront of what's new and hot, the water bearer will also introduce you to avant-garde music and art.

Written in the Stars
Attending a Star Trek convention or having an *X-Files* marathon at home are things that a water bearer will enjoy. Since he is always keyed in to the latest trends, he will also love attending a music festival or gallery opening.

However, because your Aquarius pal is so focused on the future, he tends to be unreliable. Additionally, because he is an air sign, he daydreams quite a bit, especially about his latest ideas. This explains why he frequently misses appointments and shows up late to parties. While it's easy to get irritated with his flakiness, remember it is not a reflection of how much (or little) he cares. Chalk it up to his absentminded mad professor tendencies.

Headstrong and Hardhearted

As a fixed sign, Aquarius doesn't like when others disagree with him—mostly because he always believes he's right. Your Aquarius friend likes to come across as an expert on the subject, even when he's not. Because the water bearer is so attached to his opinions and ideas, he can come across as a know-it-all. Debates and discussions with him can be frustrating, as even when he is proven wrong, he will continue to say he is right. His inherent rebel heart causes him to be defiant just for the sake of being defiant. While this stubbornness is undoubtedly vexing at times, friends may find Aquarius's commitment to his ideas inspiring—that is, if they want to save themselves from engaging in an argument. His hardheadedness is also useful when he goes to bat for you, which he is often known to do.

While your Aquarius friend is dedicated to your friendship, however, he may often come across as neutral and detached. He prefers to be an impartial observer in most situations, to the point where he seems almost devoid of emotion. This is because Aquarius distrusts emotions; he believes they only cloud your judgment and ability to think rationally. Additionally, the water bearer's need for freedom and personal space means he doesn't like feeling tied down. As a result, he will distance himself from friendships at times when he feels trapped or smothered. If you haven't heard from Aquarius for a few days, give him the space he needs; he'll come back around when he's feeling more communicative and open. It's important to realize that deep down inside, while Aquarius might act aloof, he feels quite attached. If he considers you a friend, know that his detached nature hides a warm heart.

The Quirky One: Where You'll Meet Aquarius

Because Aquarius is all about helping out others, he prides himself on being the champion of the underdogs. You'll often meet him working at a not-for-profit organization or volunteering at the local soup kitchen. The water bearer often works as a teacher, either in a school environment, or in an unusual leisure activity like fencing or puppeteering. Aquarius is actually known for his many (often uncommon) hobbies. And when he taps into his creative side, he enjoys experimental theater or poetry classes. As the sci-fi lover he is, you could also meet Aquarius at a sci-fi convention or UFO-sighting meeting. Passionate for all things related to science and technology, Aquarius may pop up on your radar as a researcher, engineer, or electronics store employee. Always up for a challenge, the water bearer is also drawn to death-defying sports like skydiving, rock climbing, or skiing.

You'll recognize Aquarius by his friendly and quirky yet elusive disposition. He is the brainy conversationalist who always asks the most interesting questions. Even when the discussion seems to be over, Aquarius will keep probing deeper into the subject, regardless of whether he's the only one left talking—which makes him all the more fascinating.

Talking Tech: How to Become Friends with Aquarius

A sociable creature, Aquarius is a gifted conversationalist with a friendly disposition. However, while he is perfectly congenial to others, he initially does better with groups of people than one-on-one. This is because Aquarius is a deeply cautious person, as well as a thinker rather than a feeler, which causes him to come across as aloof, sometimes even cold. He needs to appeal to logic to understand someone or something, while others (such as water signs) may prefer to tap into emotions to shed light on what is happening. Being too direct, or coming off too strong, will only cause the water bearer to retreat. Entice him by discussing topics related to science, technology, and humanitarian issues. Admire his smartphone (chances are he'll have the latest edition) or inquire about his many hobbies and love for books. Above all, reveal your quirky side to Aquarius; he likes people and things that are different. Give him time to get to know you and trust you. If you prove yourself to be offbeat and honest, with great intellect, you'll have a long-lasting friendship with Aquarius.

Suffocating and Judgmental: Aquarius Friendship Dislikes

Aquarius doesn't do clingy friends. He prefers people who are independent and have their own varied interests and passions—just like he does. Aquarius needs his space to explore his calling and enjoy all of his hobbies, and if he feels smothered by a friend, he will have no trouble ghosting them. By the same token, because the water bearer knows he's a bit different from everyone else, he needs to feel accepted and supported for who he is. If he feels unsupported or judged at any point in a friendship, he will walk away.

Analytical Arguer: How Aquarius Handles Conflict

As the "Can't we all just get along?" humanitarian of the zodiac, Aquarius doesn't like the feeling of anger. This means he does everything in his power to avoid or control it. For example, he will go for a walk to calm down, take a time-out in his car, or ignore a conflict altogether in order to keep the peace. Aquarius refuses to let his temper get the best of him. However, if a conflict arises that cannot be avoided, he will do whatever it takes to talk out the problem. Aquarius needs to understand why a conflict happened, and will dissect it in order to figure out how you can both get what you need and want out of the situation. He will search for brand-new ways to find a solution—anything to avoid this unpleasant argument from reoccurring in the future.

If you do find yourself in an argument with your Aquarius friend, it's best to present your side as clearly and factually as possible. He doesn't do well with emotions; in fact, your tears will only further complicate the matter. While he doesn't like to give in easily, if an agreement cannot be reached, chances are the water bearer will be the first one to wave his white flag so the conflict can be resolved as swiftly as possible. But don't let Aquarius's peacemaking ways fool you: if pushed, he will lash out with his sharp tongue. And while he might not outwardly express emotion, he hurts deeply. If you've managed to wound your Aquarius friend, expect him to cut you out of his life, no questions asked.

Space and Security: Maintaining Your Friendship with Aquarius

Aquarius likes to be of service in some capacity. Whether it's spreading his knowledge or lending a hand, he loves feeling useful. Don't hesitate to ask for his assistance, whether you need help setting up for an event, troubleshooting your new laptop, or solving a puzzle. He'll appreciate that you asked.

Your Aquarius friend is also inherently independent and needs to be on his own sometimes. By respecting his space, you're offering him a valuable gift that will mean the world to him.

Additionally, while the water bearer can be quite deep and analytical a lot of the time, he has one of the most wicked senses of humor in the zodiac. However, sometimes he requires a gentle nudge from a friend in order to lighten up and have some good old-fashioned fun. Crack a joke and encourage him to let loose, and neither of you will regret it.

At the heart of Aquarius, however, is his secret sense of insecurity. He's often reserved or aloof because he fears he won't be accepted or loved for who he is—when all he truly longs for is exactly that. Of course, he doesn't want people to know this. So when your Aquarius friend is acting distant, reassure him how much you appreciate him. In fact, pull him in a giant bear hug and hold him in tight. Just don't let on that you know he is feeling insecure.

> **BFF Bonus Points**
>
> When it comes to gifts, Aquarius rules friendship, so selecting an attractive friendship ring or bracelet, or a framed photograph of the two of you, will be much appreciated. As the future tripper of the zodiac, your water bearer friend will also love a sci-fi graphic novel or membership to a planetarium.

Friendship Compatibility

What makes Gemini a great match for Aquarius? Why might Aquarius find it difficult to bond with Pisces? The following section delves into each of Aquarius's friendship compatibility matches, as well as how he operates in a friendship with each sign that doesn't fall within his key matches.

Aquarius and Aries

These two independent, trailblazing signs have a lot in common. They both love adventures, and have a penchant for risk-taking. Daring activities like skydiving or parasailing are something they will enjoy doing together. However, both Aquarius and Aries are stubborn, which means someone will have to give in sometimes—with Aquarius doing more than his fair share. Regardless, while the water bearer might grow tired of the ram's bossiness, and the ram may accuse Aquarius of being a martyr, these signs have a lot of fun together.

Aquarius and Taurus

While on the surface Aquarius and Taurus might not have a lot in common, they both have a deep-seated desire for loyalty and security, and love their friends tremendously. While the water bearer balks at the bull's excessive indulgence, and the bull doesn't understand the water bearer's frequent need to be around large groups of people, they will get along swimmingly when working with each other one-on-one, especially on a creative project.

When Stars Align

Aquarius doesn't usually treat himself to luxuries. However, he will welcome a surprise treat from Taurus (who knows just how to spoil a friend), like a trip to a spa or a dinner at a fancy restaurant.

Aquarius and Gemini

Aquarius and Gemini have a special bond. Inquisitive Gemini is charmed by the eccentric Aquarius, while Aquarius admires Gemini's clever mind. These two social air signs love palling around together, and never run out of things to talk about. While Aquarius may grow weary of Gemini's flakiness, and Gemini will bemoan Aquarius's rigidness, these signs have enough in common to overcome these criticisms and continue laughing together for a long time.

Aquarius and Cancer

This friendship may have trouble taking off at first. In fact, these two are very different people with different needs and perspectives on life. Aquarius can be uncomfortable with Cancer's emotional nature, and Cancer may feel irritated by Aquarius's aloofness. However, Aquarius can help expand Cancer's world, and Cancer can help Aquarius become more in touch with his feelings. Focusing on each other's strengths and what the other sign brings to the friendship will make it easier for them to see eye to eye.

Aquarius and Leo

Aquarius and Leo have opposing energies that can be a bit challenging to overcome. Leo's "me first" attitude rubs the humanitarian Aquarius the wrong way, while Aquarius can be too deep for fun-loving Leo. However, if Aquarius can help Leo see the bigger picture, and Leo can warm up Aquarius's cool exterior, this friendship can grow. Each sign will need to see the other's differences as strengths and not criticize them.

Aquarius and Virgo

Aquarius and Virgo can change the world together when they join forces. The water bearer's big dreams have the potential to come to life thanks to the practicality of the virgin. Both analytical, they also appreciate and understand the other's perspective on life and how the other gets things done. And because both are naturally introverted, they don't take the other's aloofness personally. While Virgo can be too fussy for Aquarius, and Aquarius's rebellious streak can make the virgin uncomfortable, they form a great team.

Aquarius and Libra

These two signs adore each other. Both sociable creatures, Aquarius and Libra love hitting the town together, and can talk into the wee hours about current headlines and politics. Aquarius appreciates Libra's diplomacy, while Libra is taken by Aquarius's eccentric personality. Though Libra can be too clingy at times for independent Aquarius, and Aquarius's aloofness can frustrate affectionate Libra, their friendship can withstand the test of time.

Aquarius and Scorpio

While Aquarius and Scorpio think they can make a difference in each other's lives, it may be these inherent differences that drive them apart. The scorpion's secretive nature will annoy Aquarius, while Aquarius's busy social calendar will ignite jealousy in Scorpio. Additionally, both are stubborn (due to being fixed signs), and neither will yield to the other for anything—not even which movie to watch. If each sign can appreciate the other's unique demeanor, it may be enough to keep this friendship strong.

> **When Stars Align**
> Scorpio needs to accept Aquarius's eccentricities if these signs are going to form a solid friendship. Any attempt at criticism will cause the water bearer to swiftly flee to the next friend.

Aquarius and Sagittarius

Aquarius and Sagittarius are like family. They're both free spirits who long for independence and endless adventures. The water bearer appreciates the archer's optimism, while the archer digs the rebelliousness of the water bearer. They are excellent travel companions, and can make even the dullest experience seem like the most amazing time ever. These two signs are so tight, in fact, that Aquarius can overlook Sagittarius's bluntness, and Sagittarius can easily ignore Aquarius's cold exterior. There are many laughs and heartfelt talks to be had that will further cement this joyful connection.

Aquarius and Capricorn

Avant-garde meets old school when Aquarius and Capricorn come together. The water bearer is all about the trendiest events and going to underground concerts, while the sea goat prefers to stay home and play board games. Though there will be a few challenges to overcome, these two do enjoy spending time with each other. Aquarius appreciates Capricorn's thoughtfulness, and Capricorn values Aquarius's ambitious visions. If they can open each other up to new ways of living life, they will make many memories together.

Aquarius and Aquarius

When two water bearers come together, they're basically one person. These friends love spending together, whether they're discussing conspiracy theories, watching a sci-fi movie, or helping out the less fortunate. While their shared stubbornness may bring them to loggerheads at times, their reticence to arguing means they're able to skip over any disagreements with ease. This friendship is also bound for endless adventures, as they support each other's biggest dreams.

Aquarius and Pisces

While these two aren't frenemies, they may not exactly be best buddies either. Aquarius may be too intellectual and unemotional for the sensitive and daydreaming Pisces, and Pisces's clinginess can frustrate the independent Aquarius. However, these two compassionate signs will come together for charity events, and also like discussing spiritual topics with each other.

Friendship Planets: Venus and Jupiter

Looking at the planets of Venus and Jupiter in your friend's and your charts, in addition to the Sun signs, can help you gain a better understanding of your friend and your friendship with them. The sensual planet Venus rules love and unions of all kinds, including friendships. Its location in your birth chart indicates *how* you love. Jupiter, the planet of optimism, success, and generosity, indicates how you *show* your love to those close to you. Its influence nudges you to experience new things in life, and to be generous with others.

Venus in Aquarius

Venus in Aquarius has a kind and loving nature that defies convention. A freethinker who embraces his uniqueness, he thrives on new experiences and looks for the same in his friends. However, while he is friendly and kindhearted, he may appear aloof at times. This coldness stems from his innate logical nature and distrust of emotions; he fears emotions will interfere with his brilliant decision-making skills.

Venus in Aquarius also tends to have many friends from different groups or clubs, since he has an array of hobbies. However, he still needs to balance this extroversion with alone time in order to unwind and recharge. He values personal freedom more than anything, which may interfere with his friendships. Friends might not understand why he often needs to go it alone, which is why it's a good idea for him to make a habit of regularly staying in touch with his inner circle so they know how much he appreciates them. After all, Venus in Aquarius has an unwavering sense of loyalty to his friends—which they in turn value him for. They also love him for his fair and nonjudgmental nature, as well as his ease with speaking his mind on just about any topic. When it comes to selecting those for his tried-and-true tribe, he can't tolerate those who cling to him, and will walk away as quickly as possible from any drama.

Jupiter in Aquarius

Jupiter in Aquarius has a magnetic personality that has the ability to attract and win over many friends from many different walks of life. He is mentally adventurous and loves challenging his friends, whether it's through debating world politics or figuring out a puzzle. His impartiality and open-mindedness are also refreshing to others, which is why he is able to get along so well with so many people.

Jupiter in Aquarius's expansive mind also inspires his friends to think outside of the box, while his sense of camaraderie helps connect people to work together on projects, especially those relating to humanitarian issues. He loves sharing his unique thoughts and experiences with his friends, from what the twenty-second century might look like, to his time spent climbing Mount Everest. However, Jupiter in Aquarius also has a tendency to ignore other people's opinions and can be unflinching when it comes to his own ideas. He has a strong need to be right, which can turn off his nearest and dearest. It's important for him to respect his friends' feelings and views, especially if they differ from his own. It's in these moments, too, that reverting to his sharp sense of humor could help ease any tension.

Chapter 12

Pisces
(February 19–March 20)

Pisces is a good-natured, sensitive soul who's probably a little psychic. Okay, a lot psychic. As the last sign in the zodiac, the otherworldly Pisces embodies characteristics of the other signs, which allows her to connect deeply with everyone she meets. She's the friend who constantly texts you after your breakup to make sure you're all right, and shows up at your house with chicken soup when you're sick.

The Dreamer

Chances are your Pisces friend is one of the most reflective people you know. She probably owns a library of diaries, which she has continually filled since she was small. Her insightful nature is in part because she is symbolized by the two entwined fish, which represent hidden depths and the connection between the conscious and subconscious. She is the friend who you can't quite figure out at times.

Ruled by Neptune, the planet of inspiration, dreams, and illusion, Pisces is the esoteric and spiritually evolved friend who would rather ponder life than live it. She is always daydreaming, struggling between what's real and what simply exists in her vivid imagination. She constantly reviews where she's been, and dreams of where she wants to go next. In doing so, she also deliberates between her strengths and weaknesses, including dealing with her "shadow self": the subconscious part of a person that includes desires, fears, and impulses—everything that is usually hidden from others (and even at times from that individual). Pisces believes that in understanding her deepest self, she is able to live more freely—that is, whenever she stops daydreaming (because Pisces can daydream for hours).

Your Pisces friend's woolgathering can be inspiring, giving you the motivation to look inward yourself, potentially healing old wounds and prompting aha moments. Don't be surprised if you and your Pisces pal create vision boards or journal together. As a water sign who feels her way through the world, getting lost in long discussions about emotions is another favorite Piscean activity, so if you ever need to get something off your chest, your Pisces friend will be only too happy to lend an ear. There is no shame when it comes to revealing feelings in Pisces's world.

Written in the Stars

When traveling, Pisces enjoys destinations that are surrounded by her natural habitat: water. And because she loves to let her mind wander, she prefers low-key locales where she can lounge and relax. Think Jamaica, Phuket, or Hawaii.

Of course, being so connected to her subconscious is why your fish friend has such an active imagination. Her ability to tap into a far-out creative space makes her one of the most innovative artists of the zodiac. If you need help coming up with an idea for a creative project, Pisces will give you ten. The flip side of her constantly fantasizing and imagining romantic cinematic scenes (Pisces is, after all, the dreamer of the zodiac) is that drama seems to follow her around everywhere. Unlike Leo, Pisces doesn't intend to be the drama queen (or king); she just can't help but want to make (or force) her fantasies into reality, even if it results in an unhappy ending.

The Healer

As an emotional and intuitive water sign, your Pisces friend is so sensitive that she's prone to absorbing the energies of others. She may even have a collection of healing crystals, sage, or anything else that might help her ward off negative energy. Intensely perceptive, Pisces can pick up on what you're feeling before you even say a word. Her telepathic-like powers especially come in handy when she is helping others, which is a regular pastime for the compassionate fish. Before you even shed one tear, your Pisces friend will be bringing you a tissue and offering a hug. She uses her immense capacity for empathy not only to see things from your perspective, but also to do whatever she can to support you. Pisces will drop everything to be there for her friends, often to the extent of prioritizing others' needs over her own. While her vulnerability can be jarring at times, especially to those friends who can't readily access their emotions, it may help you become more comfortable with owning and expressing your own feelings, which can be incredibly healing.

Written in the Stars

As a water sign, Pisces benefits from activities that involve water. They help her reconnect with or better express her emotions when she may be feeling overwhelmed or confused by them. While she's not an overly active sign, she does enjoy swimming, surfing, snorkeling, or sailing.

Full of otherworldly wisdom, Pisces is also known for being an old soul. Couple that with her ability to identify and empathize with just about anyone, and it's no wonder your Pisces friend is the sage counselor who almost everyone turns to for advice and a shoulder to cry on. If there's a wound to address, Pisces will do everything in her power to heal it.

Pisces Quirks: The Flexible Fish

As a mutable sign (meaning she was born during the transition from one season—winter—to another—spring), the fish goes with the flow. Her laid-back nature means she is always up for trying something new. Pisces loves partying with her friends as much as she enjoys spending a quiet night in watching movies. Being mutable also means that she easily adapts to the people around her. She's as comfortable with her Wall Street friends as she is with her wallflower friends—and she'll dress the part too. And if there's a change in the Friday night dinner plans? No biggie. If you suddenly have a hankering for Italian cuisine, she'll roll with it—even if she already had lasagna the night before.

Because she is so changeable, your Pisces friend tends to be inconsistent. Don't bother leaving your plans up to the fish; she would rather have things just happen naturally and spontaneously. No wonder she is always late! Instead of relying on time to get her through the day, Pisces relies on her whims, which can be tricky when trying to schedule just about anything with her.

However, if you need a last-minute wing-person at a charity event, or at a party where you know your ex will show up, Pisces will drop everything to be there.

People-Pleaser and Pity Partier

Pisces's flexibility stems from her desire to make other people happy. If you're happy, so is she. In fact, Pisces has a hard time saying the word *no*, because she never wants to hurt anyone's feelings or create tension. This means she prefers to defer to her friends to make decisions and lead the way. This shape-shifting tendency might make others question whether they really know who Pisces is and what *she* wants. Her indecisiveness can also be frustrating for those who resent being the one to constantly make decisions and come up with the plans. Additionally, Pisces's teeter-tottering and complying nature sets her up to be taken advantage of by others. In turn, her friends might feel protective of their impressionable fish friend, which can become a point of contention as they start to feel as though they have to babysit her.

However, for all of her people-pleasing ways, your Pisces friend is fiercely protective of her squad. Her gentle nature can instantly turn defensive, and she will go to war with someone who has hurt a member of her tribe. And speaking of hurt, when Pisces's feelings get hurt, you're in for quite a meltdown. Pisces embodies melodrama like no other when she feels scorned in any way—which can be a frequent occurrence due to her extreme sensitivity. While you might try to soothe her, most of the time Pisces just needs to get the tears out of her system. The delicate fish can get so overwhelmed by her feelings, and the feelings she absorbs from those around her, that she becomes despondent. Feeling sad is a natural state in Pisces's world and, as such, pity parties are a regular occurrence. It's normal for her to need to withdraw from the world and be alone with her feelings so she can mope and have a good cry in peace. So if your Pisces friend disappears for a while, understand this is a part of her emotional process, and give her some much-needed space.

Living the Dream: Where You'll Meet Pisces

Pisces is strongly motivated by the desire to fulfill her many dreams, which means you'll most likely meet the fish anywhere that fits within her life vision. Often heeding her creative side, she'll likely be found expressing the inner workings of her artistic soul, from attending art galleries to taking dance classes to visiting the theater.

BFF Bonus Points

When surprising your Pisces friend with a gift, tap into her creative side with a blank canvas and set of paints, concert tickets, or a new journal. As a water sign, she'll also appreciate new swimwear, wax for her surfboard, or a swanky reusable water bottle.

Her deep well of empathy will also draw her to any activity or job that helps others, like nursing, teaching, or volunteering at a food bank. Being around animals is also incredibly healing to Pisces, as she finds the day-to-day elements of socializing and subconsciously absorbing the energies of other people to be overwhelming. When spending time with animals, she is able to just *be* and let go of all of the emotions she has soaked up during the day. After all, whether they mean to or not, friends transfer their problems onto Pisces, while animals just want to play and cuddle. Thus, it's likely you'll bump into Pisces at a petting zoo, animal shelter, or veterinarian office. As a water sign, Pisces can also be found lazing at the beach, lounging by the pool, or engaging in a water sport like windsurfing.

You'll recognize Pisces by her carefree, positive attitude and her sympathetic vibe. She is the one who is listening to everyone's problems and laughing at everyone's jokes.

Opening Up: How to Become Friends with Pisces

While Pisces is naturally introverted, her gentle and friendly demeanor makes her very approachable. Though she is great at reading people, including whether or not you'll make a good BFF, you can still get her attention by sparking an interesting conversation, especially regarding arts and entertainment topics, such as books and celebrities. Additionally, if you engage her in a discussion about spirituality and mysticism, you'll win her attention for hours.

Revealing your vulnerable side is also something Pisces will appreciate. Open up to her, and she'll instantly feel a connection with you. Make her laugh, and you'll put her at ease. Above all, Pisces is looking for a friend who is an artist and dreamer like she is. Respect her emotional nature and need for solitude, and you'll have a friend in this fish for life.

Emotionally Unavailable: Pisces Friendship Dislikes

While Pisces tries to get along with just about everyone, she has a hard time warming up to those who are closed off emotionally. Emotional support is vital to her, which is why she prefers friends who respect emotions and who aren't afraid to express their own feelings. Stability in her friendships is also important to Pisces. Someone who flits in and out of her life and has trouble staying in touch will only hurt the sensitive fish, so she would rather pull the plug on a friendship early than have her feelings hurt later.

Playing the Blame Game: How Pisces Handles Conflict

Your Pisces friend really doesn't want to fight. Her sensitive nature means conflict makes her feel uneasy, and she will do anything to avoid confrontation. So if she does pick a fight with you, consider it significant.

However, even while arguing, Pisces would rather blame herself than attempt to disparage you. She'll also easily express how she feels, and why she feels it, in an attempt to smooth things over as quickly as possible. An emotional sign, Pisces will appreciate the same in return; she does better with emotions than she does with logic and cold hard facts. Stating things in terms of "I feel" rather than "I think" is the best way to resolve an issue with the fish. Validating her feelings is also important to Pisces, and will swiftly bring things to a more peaceful state.

While your Pisces friend wants to stay friends forever, once hurt, she has a difficult time forgiving and forgetting. Rather than getting angry, though, the fish will be disappointed in you, which can be far more cutting.

Action and Affection: Maintaining Your Friendship with Pisces

Pisces feels everything deeply—more deeply in fact than any other sign. This includes sadness. While respecting your fish pal's need for space during one of her blue moments will go a long way, it will also mean the world to her if you offer your own shoulder for her to cry on. Pisces often forgets that she, too, needs a support system; reminding her she already has one will make a huge difference in her life. Showing you care even when she isn't feeling down will also go a long way. You can make her day by texting her an "I miss you" text, or sending a birthday or get-well card. A great big bear hug is also a great option.

Pisces is also secretly very hard on herself. One of the most serious obstacles she faces in life is the struggle to overcome failure. She tends to mentally revisit her losses over and over again, making little headway with her to-do list. Offering practical advice as well as support and encouragement will mean so much to her.

Your Pisces friend also has big dreams, but since she spends so much of her time in her fantasy life, she sometimes fails to take action in her real life. This is often because her dreams are so overwhelming to her that she fears the outcome will never live up to the images she's created on her vision board. Helping your Pisces pal come up with a solid plan of action will enable her to see her dreams through to reality.

Friendship Compatibility

How can the two very different signs of Pisces and Aries ever see eye to eye? What makes Cancer the perfect support system for Pisces? In the following section, you will discover each of Pisces's Sun sign matches, as well as how she might forge deep connections with signs that aren't within her main compatibility matches.

Pisces and Aries

This is an oil and water combination. Oil being the fiery Aries, and water being the flowing Pisces. However, Aries will encourage Pisces to experience new adventures in life, and in return, Aries's creativity will be influenced greatly by Pisces. Of course,

Aries's bossiness can intimidate Pisces, and Pisces's indecision will irritate Aries. Agreeing on plans will also be complicated, given the opposing energies of these signs. However, they can have a lot of fun together if they learn to accept each other for who they are.

Pisces and Taurus

While they might seem like opposites, the fish and the bull are essentially peanut butter and jelly. Pisces appreciates the grounding energy of Taurus whenever her emotions get the best of her, and Taurus values the laid-back vibe of Pisces. Together, they will love watching movies or trying out the latest restaurant in town. While Pisces may get frustrated with Taurus's inherent need to be practical, especially when emotions are involved, and Taurus may be irked by Pisces's constant need for deep discussions, these two will easily overlook their differences because their bond is so strong.

Pisces and Gemini

The fish and the twin like making each other laugh, but there's more silliness than substance to this duo. Gemini's chaotic energy can be too overwhelming for Pisces, and Pisces's constant daydreaming is a mystery to Gemini. While they like discussing current events together, Gemini's fickleness will annoy Pisces, and Pisces's roller-coaster emotions will drive Gemini bananas. With Gemini's intellect and Pisces's creativity, however, they can connect well when working on a project together.

Pisces and Cancer

These two feel *all* the feels when they're together. Both emotional creatures, Pisces and Cancer feel safe and secure in expressing whatever they're feeling—which is a lot—with each other. The nurturing crab loves sending pick-me-up texts to the fish whenever she's feeling down, and the fish is adept at drawing the homebody crab out of her shell to attend the latest party. While Cancer's ambition may baffle Pisces, and Pisces's impracticality may confuse Cancer, these two form a wonderful support system that will stand the test of time.

When Stars Align

Pisces and Cancer are so intuitively connected that they often know how the other is feeling and what they're thinking without uttering a word. One look says a lot for these friendship soul mates.

Pisces and Leo

This is an interesting pair. While introverted Pisces can feel overshadowed by the sociable Leo, and Leo is confounded by Pisces's sometimes reclusive tendencies, they both have a deep appreciation for art, from watching a movie to attending a play. Though the fish's sensitivity can be too much to bear at times for the fun-loving lion, and the lion's brash nature can annoy the calming fish, these kindhearted souls can form a loving connection.

Pisces and Virgo

As astrological opposites, the dreamy Pisces and the practical Virgo may appear to not get along. However, they soon find that their differences balance each other out. The fish welcomes the virgin's rational advice, while the virgin feels supported by the fish to fully be herself and express her feelings. Both are service-oriented signs, so they'll also enjoy doing volunteer work together. Afterward, these two introverts will split a pot of tea at a secluded café and toast to their surprising friendship.

Pisces and Libra

Pisces and Libra can become good friends—if they make the decision to do so. As the two most indecisive signs of the zodiac, it's difficult to get anything done between them. They can't even choose which movie to watch on Saturday night. It's their inherent disparities that may drive them apart if they are not patient. Libra's an intellectual who depends on logic, while Pisces navigates the world through her feelings. The fish's neediness and the scales' need for social freedom could sink this connection if they cannot accept their differences.

Pisces and Scorpio

Pisces and Scorpio form a freeing connection that is both fun and comforting for each. The fish provides emotional safety for the scorpion, while the scorpion makes the fish feel protected. They can tell each other their deepest secrets and reveal their rawest feelings in absolute confidence. Both highly creative people, Pisces and Scorpio also love collaborating on creative projects together, and, as water signs, they'll also enjoy swimming and lounging on the beach together.

Pisces and Sagittarius
Both Pisces and Sagittarius are spontaneous signs who enjoy acting on impulse—like going on a last-minute road trip. However, the fish may feel too much for the active archer (who prefers to get out and do things rather than dream about them). On the other hand, Pisces may feel put off by Sagittarius's brash attitude, so disagreements are bound to occur. However, they can indulge in long philosophical discussions, finding common ground in their interest in spirituality.

Pisces and Capricorn
These are two very different signs that somehow just get each other. Whimsical Pisces inspires the practical Capricorn to take creative chances, while Capricorn helps Pisces make decisions. The vulnerability of the fish also draws out the inner sensitivity of the sea goat, and the sea goat admires the loyalty given by the fish. While Capricorn might grow tired of Pisces's emotional outbursts, and Pisces may get annoyed with her Capricorn friend's stubbornness, there is mainly smooth sailing ahead for these two.

After a disappointment, Capricorn can cheer up Pisces with a collection of rom-com movies, chocolates, and a box of tissues—while also remembering to keep her "I told you so" comments to herself.

Pisces and Aquarius

Each sign's inherent uniqueness and love for deep spiritual discussions will help cement the friendship between Pisces and Aquarius. They both admire and accept the other's eccentricities, and enjoy working together on a charity project. However, the water bearer's aloofness will confound the fish, while the fish's sentimentality may annoy the water bearer. In the end, Pisces may be too insecure to accept the Aquarius's flitting ways, and Aquarius may find Pisces too needy for a lasting friendship.

Pisces and Pisces

While the two fish greatly appreciate each other's immense sensitivity and creativity, there may be too much dreaminess between these friends to keep their bond steady on the ground. Being prone to emotional breakdowns, along with their shared indecisiveness, inevitability leads to conflict, which both Pisces are deeply uncomfortable with. They both enjoy working on artistic projects and discussing spiritual topics together; however, they will need to avoid sinking into mutual despondence and negativity, as misery loves company.

Friendship Planets: Venus and Jupiter

Considering the planets of Venus and Jupiter in your friend's and your charts, in addition to your Sun signs, can help you gain a better understanding of your friend and your friendship with them. Venus rules love and unions of all kinds, including friendships. It indicates *how* you love. The planet of optimism, success, and generosity, Jupiter indicates how you *show* that love to those you care about. Its influence nudges you to experience new things in life, and to be generous with others.

Venus in Pisces

Venus in Pisces is most definitely a lover, not a fighter. She is a dreamy, kindhearted, and gentle soul, and it's easy for her to form connections. Her big heart and sympathetic ear make her friends seek her out when they're going through a tough time. They know she'll listen without judgment and will help them explore and express their deepest feelings. Her compassion for others is almost limitless, and she loves lending a helping hand when others are in need. She has an extraordinary ability to empathize with people, which is both a blessing and a curse. It is a blessing because she has such easy access to her emotions—a curse for the same reason. In fact, it's easy for her to become overwhelmed by her feelings, which is why she often retreats from the outside world and seeks solitude in order to recharge her batteries.

Escapism comes naturally to Venus in Pisces, and she'll often go MIA for days, lost in her own world. Because her friends might not understand her need to withdraw, it's important for her to let them know where she is and why. She also spends a lot of time daydreaming, thanks to her active imagination. The artistic results of her imagination are something that she loves to share with her nearest and dearest in the form of poetry, handwritten notes, and creative projects. As much as she loves to support her friends, however, it's also important for Venus in Pisces to set personal boundaries, especially since she tends to adapt to others, often losing herself in the process.

Jupiter in Pisces

Jupiter in Pisces is a positive, hopeful person who believes there is a greater purpose than what meets the eye. She is in touch with her feelings and the feelings of others, and she believes that people are most connected to one another through their vulnerability. She encourages her friends to explore the inner workings of their souls, and provides them with a safe space where they are free to express themselves. She likes to bond with her friends through meditation, quiet walks on the beach, or yoga classes—anything that helps promote intimacy rather than superficiality.

Jupiter in Pisces is her best self when she is serving others, whether it's through humanitarian organizations, religious work, or even politics. Her friends are inspired by how easily she walks on the path of enlightenment, and her openness to others' unique views motivates them to try to be as accepting. While she embodies an idealistic energy that's certainly contagious, however, it's easy for her to become disappointed when friends act out of turn. It's essential for her to remain grounded and realistic when it comes to her expectations in order to avoid a letdown.

Index